TEAM
TEACHING
WHAT, WHY, AND HOW?

FRANCIS J. BUCKLEY, S.J.

Sage Publications, Inc.
International Educational and Professional Publisher
Thousand Oaks ■ London ■ New Delhi

For information:

 Sage Publications, Inc.
2455 Teller Road
Thousand Oaks, California 91320
E-mail: order@sagepub.com

Sage Publications Ltd.
6 Bonhill Street
London EC2A 4PU
United Kingdom

Sage Publications India Pvt. Ltd.
M-32 Market
Greater Kailash I
New Delhi 110 048 India

Printed in the United States of America

Library of Congress Cataloging-in-Publication Data

Buckley, Francis J.
   Team teaching: What, why, and how? / by Francis J. Buckley.
      p. cm.
   Includes bibliographical references and index.

   ISBN 0-7619-0744-0 (pbk.: acid-free paper)
   1. Teaching teams. 2. Teaching teams—Planning. 3. Teaching. 4.
Teaching—Planning. I. Title.
   LB1029.T4 B83   1999
   371.14´8—dc21   98-40297

This book is printed on acid-free paper.

   01   02   03   04   05   06   7   6   5   4   3   2

Acquiring Editor: Jim Nageotte
Editorial Assistant: Heidi Van Middlesworth
Production Editor: Denise Santoyo
Editorial Assistant: Patricia Zeman
Typesetters: Rose Tylak/Tina Hill
Cover Designer: Candice Harman

To my friends and mentors:

Edwin McDermott, S.J.,

and Maria de la Cruz Aymes, S.H.

With deep gratitude and affection

Contents

SECTION FOUR: EVALUATION AND SUPPORT

Preface
Why Bother With This Book?

Imagine actively taking part in a psychology class taught by Freud, Adler, and Jung. Not just passively listening to Steve Allen's Classical Conversations or watching Roundtable Discussions or Bill Moyers interviewing Huston Smith or Joseph Campbell about religion. Those taped sessions garnered an audience of thousands, eventually millions. But the audience could not interrupt and ask questions of their own. They could only look and listen.

What an opportunity, to sit in a classroom over the course of a semester and enter into dialogue with

- Carl Sagan, Françoise Sagan, and Fritjof Capra as they argue about the nature of the universe
- Margaret Mead, Ruth Benedict, and a team of contemporary anthropologists differing on how to get to know and appreciate people of another culture
- Hannah Arendt with Generals MacArthur and Eisenhower and Patton analyzing World War II for a class at West Point
- Pablo Picasso, Jacques Derrida, and Ingmar Bergman discussing modern civilization with Mother Teresa

Would you want to take part in any of those sessions?

No wonder that teachers and students are excited about team teaching! All books on team teaching are out of print, but hundreds of periodical articles show a lively interest in the topic. This book will provide an overview with helpful advice. It will explain how and why team teaching works. It will try to answer questions about team teaching with a detailed and comprehensive review of research material and with practical applications, written in a clear, readable style. The nature, purpose, types, history, and evaluation of team teaching will be covered. The book will also treat the resources needed and the roles of teachers, students, and administrators. It will strengthen the case of those who want to try this innovative approach, comparing and contrasting it with other teaching techniques. Its underlying premise is that two heads are better than one. Dialogue excites, electrifies. Teaching can be improved by proactive experiments instead of waiting to be forced to catch up with the advances in information, technology, and culture.

The primary goal of shifting from individual instruction to a team is to improve the quality of teaching and learning. Team teaching is but one of many means to that end, but a very important step along the road of constantly adjusting the educational system to the changing needs of students and abilities of teachers.

Implementing a team approach is not a simple affair. It will involve faculty, administration, support staff, and students. It will raise issues of management style, interpersonal relations, and educational goals and methods. It will directly affect scheduling, classroom sizes, and budgeting. Indirectly, it will affect instructional media support, faculty and student morale, retention, and recruitment. The chain reaction will change the entire school environment.

Are the results worth the effort? Emphatically, yes.

Our thinking frequently is culture bound. Western European and American cultures are highly individualistic, often excessively so. There is good reason to treasure academic freedom. It protects professors with totally new and seemingly outlandish approaches, questions, and ideas. But academic freedom can flourish in classrooms where teachers publicly disagree and model courteous discourse to their students. African and primal societies often welcome teams of shamans or medicine men/women or healers, experts in the lore of that culture, to roll back the forces of ignorance. Middle Eastern and Asian cultures recognize the value of combining insights from several sources in the search for wisdom. Extended families enable children to learn from several teachers simultaneously. All teachers can learn from these cultures.

Business, sports, space exploration, and medicine have stressed the value of teamwork. These values are brought to academia in the form of team teaching.

To meet the common objection, "It won't work in my field," a bibliography of articles and books will provide theory and examples. They show how it can be used by administrators and teachers in a variety of disciplines, in formal and informal settings, and with different age and cultural groups to improve teaching.

The primary audience of this book will be college teachers and administrators, graduate and undergraduate, in all disciplines, particularly those interested in innovative and effective teaching. It should also be helpful to librarians, teachers, and administrators below the college level.

This book is the fruit of team teaching in a variety of formats for 30 years, from elementary to graduate school, in religious education and anthropology, sociology, and psychology at the University of San Francisco. Personal care for students and openness to new ideas and techniques have been hallmarks of Jesuit education for over four centuries. I want to express my thanks to my colleagues and students. They have taught me much over the years. I am especially indebted to Edwin McDermott, S.J., and Maria de la Cruz Aymes, S.H. We have laughed and fought and prayed and learned with students all over the world.

SECTION ONE

General Principles

What Is Team Teaching?

Teaching is not just any kind of interaction between teachers and students. Some content is to be taught and learned: some knowledge, values, or skills, and preferably all three (Hyman, 1970, pp. 10-17).[1]

Teaching goes beyond mere conditioning or drilling by rote repetition. Neither drilling nor conditioning really aims at understanding and appreciation. As Israel Scheffler defined it, "Teaching may be characterized as an activity aimed at the achievement of learning and practised in such manner as to respect the student's intellectual integrity and capacity for independent judgment" (quoted in Hyman, 1970, p. 8).

Teaching is a process. Learning is its goal. When teaching is most successful, both students and teachers learn. If little or no learning takes place, the teaching has been unsuccessful. Failure to learn can be due to several causes:

- The teachers may be confused about the content to be covered.
- The teachers may have chosen methods unwisely.
- The students may not understand the teachers' medium of communication.
- The students may resist—out of boredom, lack of interest, psychological blocks or prejudices, physical fatigue, hunger, or distractions.

POOLING TALENTS

To address these learning problems jointly, professors pool their talents and efforts, considering content and method, communication and resistance. As partners, all can learn from watching others in action. Sharing ideas and skills enriches junior and senior faculty alike. Working with the support of a team makes teaching more positive, less threatening. "Team teaching assumes that the 'whole' of the participants, *working together,* will make a greater contribution than the 'sum' of the participants working alone" (Davis, 1966, p. 2).

Team teaching is not a subtle form of indoctrination, multiplying the number of authorities who say the same thing in order to overwhelm the students or dissuade them from dissent. Indoctrination is not genuine teaching at all (Hyman, 1970, pp. 5-6).

Rather, by acting with mutual concern, the teachers work to impart course content: knowledge, values, and skills. They try to lead the students to discover some aspects of reality, to become aware of the complexity of the relationships involved, to appreciate the beauty of this experience, and to strive joyously to master the skills of learning. In all of this, the faculty show reverence for the truth of the subject matter and respect for the dignity of students and teachers. They model the competence they try to impart, forming the students by their example of interaction as much as by their words. This is what team teaching is all about.[2]

Team teaching involves a group of instructors working purposefully, regularly, and cooperatively to help a group of students learn. As a team, the teachers work together in setting goals for a course, designing a syllabus, preparing individual lesson plans, actually teaching students together, and evaluating the results. They share insights, arguing with one another and perhaps even challenging students to decide which approach is correct. This experience is exciting. Everybody wins!

VARIATIONS ON A THEME

There is no single model or template for using team teaching in a course. A number of variables can influence the shape a teaching team can take. For example, a team may comprise experts from a single discipline or from several disciplines. It may or may not involve the supporting aid of technicians to run audiovisual and multimedia equipment. Team members may all have the same responsibility or may distribute the burden unequally.

Other criteria on which teaching teams may differ include

- Whether the team is balanced along racial, ethnic, and gender lines
- Whether the team is self-directed, coordinated, or authority directed
- The length of the course (one semester or more)
- The characteristics of the students: age, maturity, motivation, needs, interests
- Whether the instruction will occur in one language or several
- The size of the class, and whether the class always meets as a whole or in groups
- The styles of teaching employed, the approaches taken to teaching, and the technologies or techniques employed

Later chapters will describe the most important of these variables in detail. For now, bear in mind that with all these variations, team teaching cannot be one-size-fits-all. Differing needs and professional resources rule out any universal approach. The college's enrollment, the quality of its educational leadership, and planning for the best use of its human and material resources will all influence the shape of team teaching adopted at any particular school (Beggs, 1964a).

DESCRIPTIONS AND DEFINITIONS

"The most exciting class I ever taught was one I taught as part of an interdisciplinary team sponsored by the National Endowment for the Humanities. You could feel the electricity in the room." "Team teaching challenged me as well as the students." "Team members stretch one another with their insights." "Because of my experience with team teaching, I teach all of my courses differently, getting everyone involved." So say teachers who have tried team teaching—and liked it.

In some team-taught courses, one teacher handles only one or two class sessions out of an entire semester, operating the rest of the time more like a resource person or outside consultant. The regular teacher responsible for the class may or may not attend these sessions. If the result is simply a series of unintegrated lectures, it is team teaching only in the weakest sense—and not the model presented in this book. If the teachers do not meet outside class to discuss a common agenda and evaluation, no real teamwork is involved.

In this book, team teaching means that all members of the team attend several or all of the class sessions to observe, interact, question, and learn. They also meet regularly to set goals and strategies. Further, as Dean and Witherspoon (1962) have insisted, such structural features are means to an end:

> The heart of the concept of team teaching lies not in details of structure and organization but more in the essential spirit of cooperative planning, constant collaboration, close unity, unrestrained communication, and sincere sharing. It is reflected not in a group of individuals articulating together, but rather in a group which is a single, unified team. Inherent in the plan is an increased degree of flexibility, grouping policies and practices, and size of groups, and an invigorating spirit of freedom and opportunity to revamp programs to meet . . . educational needs. (quoted in Bair & Woodward, 1964, p. 22)

How is this done?

> Two or more teachers, with or without teacher aides, cooperatively plan, instruct, and evaluate one or more class groups in an appropriate instructional space and given length of time, so as to take advantage of the special competencies of the team members. (Singer, 1964, p. 13. cf. pp. 13-22)

Team teaching can start with the informal collaboration of two teachers dealing with the same group of students and evolve into a highly structured group fully supplied with staff and the necessary hardware and software and housed in a school plant designed for it. Team teaching is better understood from the inside, beginning with personal experience of it, either as a student or as a teacher. Only in this way can its potentials be explored and felt (Chamberlin, 1969, p. 39).

LONG AGO AND FAR AWAY

Team teaching is not some new fad. It has been going on for millenia.

Political debates, philosophical discussions, and deliberations of juries were found in almost all cultures. Buddhist monks and nuns argued over the central teachings of the Buddha and how to apply them to monastic life. These are all forms of adult education.

Jesus sent out his disciples in pairs to proclaim his message. Paul and Barnabas traveled and taught together. Almost all the New Testament letters mention multiple authorship: They were written by teams of missionaries to communities who shared their faith.

Long before the Christian era, Moses and Aaron had confronted Pharaoh jointly. Prophets in Israel often taught as teams, serving in sanctuaries or at court. Samuel headed a band of ecstatic prophets. Both Elijah and Elisha were associated with prophetic guilds as masters and leaders. Even individual prophets had friends who shared their ministry; like teaching assistants, they collected the prophets' words and remembered their stories. They all shared moral ideals and traditions.

This phenomenon is not confined to ancient Israel but is common in all religions. Teachers inspired by God through mystical experiences, dreams, or visions proclaimed some spiritual insight in public. Sometimes they operated as individuals, sometimes in groups—with priests or other prophets, with friends and disciples, in Egypt, Africa, India, and China.

Wisdom traditions—advice on how to live—can also be found in all cultures, East and West, from Aesop's fables to the Hindu Vedas and Upanishads. Informal teaching took place under the guidance of elders in the family or tribe. In a cooperative environment that was often playful and sometimes dangerous, youths learned survival skills through apprenticeship—hunting, gathering, planting, fighting, communicating, tool making.

More formal instruction occurred in schools, often clustered around a court or temple. Sometimes the teaching and learning remained cooperative: Brahmin gurus in India taught older students how to teach younger ones. Elsewhere, different teachers would "debate" one another, offering different sayings, commands, and prohibitions and giving different reasons. Disciples could switch between different teachers to reap the benefits of an unstructured, disorganized, competitive, and sequential kind of team teaching. Chinese scholars could learn from the followers of Confucius, Lao-Tzu, and Buddha. Athenian students could listen to Sophists, Platonists, and Aristotelians argue. In such a context, the advice was meant not simply to be memorized but to be weighed, taken to heart, and put into practice.

The dialogue format can clearly lend itself to team teaching, with opposing points of view expressed in living conversation or written composition. Plato's dialogues are disguised monologues; they alternate between ironic reduction to absurdity and inductive discovery. But the flowing interchanges between learned people in symposia were surely a form of team teaching, though not strictly academic. In Mesopotamian and other cultures far older than that of Athens, the conclusions of the discussions were open-ended.

Later on, in medieval Europe, scholastic teachers developed the dialogue format into a highly disciplined dialectical method in which opposing points of view were presented and pondered. This could degenerate into a formal "disputation" as ritualized as a Spanish bullfight or a Japanese Noh drama, a form of literary entertainment. But properly handled, the clash of ideas could spark interest, passion, and new insights. Argument has been the traditional way of learning in Hebrew yeshivas since rabbinic times.

Sometimes the very same students were regularly and deliberately exposed to discontinuous, contradictory teachings. At the end of the 17th century, the Spanish theologian Gabriel Vazquez at the University of Alcalâ in Spain would open his afternoon classes by asking, "What did the old man [Francisco Suarez] say this morning?" Then he would spend all afternoon refuting his opponent. Did Suarez and Vazquez really belong to the same teaching team? They belonged to the same department at the same university, shared the same faith, and had the same teaching goals, even methods. Both were Jesuits. But their content differed so sharply that students would pray that the two teachers would not sit on the same examination board for oral examinations. It was an odd form of teamwork, but it certainly encouraged students to think and decide rather than merely to memorize.

YESTERDAY

Andrew Bell and Joseph Lancaster in early 19th-century Britain applied the factory model of the Industrial Revolution to education, training boys to teach boys on the elementary level. Though considered a radical innovation at the time, it simply adapted to the West the monitor system that had been customary in India for thousands of years. This tentative move toward team teaching soon died out in lower schools but would later catch on in universities, especially in science laboratories.

During the 19th century, the lecture system dominated European and American universities. Students were expected to copy down verbatim each precious insight from the professor's lips. Questions were not permitted. Research papers offered opportunities to display critical analysis and imaginative synthesis. Students might argue outside class, and professors surely disagreed among themselves, but classrooms were models of decorum, of meek acquiescence and slavish note taking. Examinations focused on detailed rendering of what had been said in class.

Teachers' colleges, though despised by university faculties, did at least encourage professors and students to reflect together on the process of learning and perhaps to learn from one another in the process. As a result, graduates of these colleges were frequently far more effective in the elementary and secondary classrooms than university lecturers who had never even reflected on how to teach, let alone studied the art of teaching. University professors were expected to teach as they themselves had been taught. At best, they determined not to imitate their most boring and tedious teachers; at worst, they were not aware of alternatives.

Earlier in the 20th century, various forms of team teaching were tried successfully in elementary and secondary schools, often with new technologies, such as films, videos, and computers. Students who became familiar with the potentials of team teaching naturally expected to find something similar on the college level. The seeds of change had been planted.

Meanwhile, a sense of professionalism was growing among university faculties. A common commitment to academic freedom was addressed by the American Association of University Professors. Concern about job security or better salaries and fringe benefits led to faculty unions. Added to this was an increasing sense of responsibility to both the academic field and the students. Professional societies flourished—and teachers began asking whether they might teach more successfully. American pragmatism encouraged them to experiment, assess results, and try again with new methods. The faculty in general were becoming ready to listen to other faculty from the department or school of education.

Finally, the trend in all academic fields to specialize into ever smaller areas had two significant results. First, professors realized the narrowness of their competence; they could not pretend to know everything. Second, there was a growing demand for general education, a sense of how all the particular facts fitted into a larger picture. Knowing their limits, university teachers became readier to share their podium with other experts from inside or outside the university. The time for team teaching had come.[3]

NOTES

1. This author provides a thorough discussion of the meaning of education.

2. Some authors prefer the term *peer coaching* to *team teaching*; see Garmston (1987), Garmston, Lindner, and Whitaker (1993), Neubert and Bratton (1987), Showers (1982, 1984), and Showers and Joyce (1996).

3. Several periodicals address issues central to team teaching: *ADE Bulletin, Childhood Education, Clearing House, College Teaching, EDRS, Education, Educational Leadership, ERIC, Journal of College Science Teaching, Journal of Educational Policy, Teaching Excellence,* and *The Professor in the Classroom.*

Why Team Teach?

The rationale for single-teacher, single-subject classes in self-contained class-rooms has been based on several misconceptions:

1. *Students all learn at the same rate.* This was never true. It is even more obviously untrue with the increase of nontraditional students. Older students learn differently. So do students ranging across a broad spectrum of cultural backgrounds and intellectual abilities.

2. *The same curricular content is appropriate for all students.* True, all students must be liberated from certain misconceptions that are common to different cultures. But this can be done in many ways. Besides, student interests differ because of background, personality, and future career plans. College education consists of more than providing information. It aims at forming values, character, habits, and skills as well. These are best formed by a variety of educational experiences that mutually enrich and reinforce one another.

3. *Periods of equal length are appropriate for all learning situations.* The sciences long ago moved away from this in laboratory courses. So did evening colleges and weekend institutes. Language and other learning laboratories are designed to provide flexible hours to meet student needs.

4. *The best class size is 30.* Most colleges have instituted large groups for lectures or films and small groups for seminars. Much depends on the kind of teaching or learning desired.

5. *The self-contained classroom provides adequate learning opportunities.* In fact, site visits, internships, and service learning formats are becoming more frequent in many fields. And virtually all college courses rely on library resources and instructional media. Use of e-mail and the Internet is growing.

6. *One teacher teaching one subject at a time works best, using the read-write-recall method.* Alas, one teacher using only one method for 40 years may show little im-

provement. The students get shortchanged (Chamberlin, 1969). Single-teacher, single-subject teaching worked well in a stable culture. Today's world demands something else. As Margaret Mead (1958) argued,

> We are no longer dealing primarily with vertical transmission of the tried and true by the old, mature, and experienced teacher to the young, immature, and inexperienced pupil in the classroom.
>
> What is needed and what we are moving toward is the inclusion of another whole dimension of learning: the lateral transmission to every sentient member of society of what has just been discovered, invented, created, manufactured, or marketed. (p. 23. cf. pp. 23-30)

Of course, team teaching is not the only answer to all problems plaguing teachers, students, and administrators. It requires planning, skilled management, willingness to risk change and even failure, humility and open-mindedness, imagination and creativity. But the results are worth it.

ADVANTAGES AND DISADVANTAGES FOR TEACHERS

Team teaching offers numerous advantages for teachers:

- Teamwork improves the quality of scholarship and teaching as various experts in the same field or different fields approach the same topic from different angles and areas of expertise: theory and practice, past and present, different gender or ethnic backgrounds. Teacher strengths are combined. Teacher weaknesses are remedied. Teachers complement one another's expertise.
- The faculty act in concert to set goals for a course, design a syllabus, prepare classes, teach students, and evaluate the results. They share insights, propose new approaches, and challenge assumptions. This promotes self-discipline and maturity in teachers and students alike.
- Teachers learn new perspectives and insights from watching one another teach. The different viewpoints suggest new approaches for research both within one field and across disciplines.
- The stimulation and challenge of team teaching prevent and remedy burnout. Boredom and mental fatigue often result from teaching the same material in the same way over and over. On a team, the individual teacher is spared from giving the same lecture to different classes. The students are grouped together for large lectures, where one professor's views are followed by another's. Students are then broken into discussion groups for deeper analysis and comparison.
- By combining classes, teachers have more time to plan lessons, improve teaching techniques, keep abreast of new developments in the field, and contact students on an individual basis.
- Increased planning keeps the syllabus current, clarifies the goals of each lesson, ensures better use of class time, and improves the quality of teaching. Teachers on a team rethink what they teach, why they teach it, and how to do it better. Lectures,

stories, audiovisuals, and demonstrations are clearer. Students are more alert and receptive. A less formal atmosphere encourages reflection and absorption as well as more focused class discussions.

- While planning, teachers can share ideas and polish materials before the class presentation. They can also budget time to discuss educational psychology, teaching techniques, and stimulating activities.
- Teachers want to teach more effectively. They also want to be energized by new approaches. Each team member invigorates the others (Weimer, 1993).
- Poor teachers can be observed, critiqued, and improved by the other team members in a nonthreatening, supportive context. The self-evaluation done by a team of teachers will be more insightful and balanced than the self-evaluation of an individual teacher.
- Teaching teams become a form of in-service training. New teachers learn from veterans. They become oriented more quickly and effectively.
- Flexibility expands. Teachers can try out different methods, class sizes, groupings, and time blocks. Specialists, consultants, and resource people are better used. Contemporary sources and applications ensure relevance.
- Morale is another important factor. Having a team to rely on significantly cuts teaching burdens and pressures. If an emergency arises—audiovisual equipment breakdown, sudden illness of a student or teacher—a team member can attend to it while the class goes on. The presence of more than one teacher also reduces student-teacher personality problems. As teachers are stretched by the team, they discover and develop new talents within themselves. Sharing in decision making boosts self-confidence. As teachers see the quality of teaching and learning improve, their self-esteem and happiness grow. This makes it easier to keep faculty and recruit newcomers.
- Team teaching provides opportunities to form and deepen friendships with peers. Planning, teaching, and evaluating together bring out many facets of the personality that might go unnoticed at department meetings.
- Team teaching provides opportunities to form and deepen friendships with students too—in a variety of contexts, in and outside class or the office, and operating as counselors as well as teachers. Student problems with alcohol or drugs, health, and family factors can all be discussed with colleagues and tentative solutions discussed. Growing awareness of such student problems and of students' special research and career interests can affect course content also.
- Team teaching applies to education what has already been found to be very valuable in industry, marketing, transportation, entertainment, and other fields. Working in teams spreads responsibility, encourages creativity, and builds community.
- Teaching in teams has been tried in many colleges and universities—and it works. (See the Bibliography for this chapter.)
- The team becomes a small group itself, with all the dynamics of interaction of personality and all the advantages that small groups bring with them.

Team teaching can also have some disadvantages for teachers:

- Probably the biggest problem is incompatible teammates. Some teachers are rigid personality types. Others are wedded to a single method. Some simply dislike the other teacher. Others are unwilling to share the spotlight or their pet ideas or to lose total control (Casey, 1964, p. 177).
- Team teaching makes more demands on time and energy. There will be inevitable inconvenience in rethinking the courses. Members must arrange mutually agreeable times for planning and evaluation sessions. Discussions can be draining, even exhausting, from the constant interaction with peers. Group decisions are slower to make.
- Some teachers do not want to risk humiliation and discouragement at the failures that may occur.
- Some faculty fear that they will be expected to do more work for the same salary.
- Some colleagues not on the team may criticize team teachers for following a fad (3,000 years old!) or for putting on airs of superiority. This can cause hurt feelings.
- Some parents and administrators can be expected to resist change of any sort.

ADVANTAGES AND DISADVANTAGES FOR STUDENTS

Some of the advantages of team teaching for students are:

- The clash of teacher viewpoints, changes of voice and rhythm, and alternation of different styles and personalities are stimulating and exciting. This gets and keeps attention and prevents boredom.
- Students discover interdependence and correlations between subject areas and between the classroom and life. Varied assignments reinforce these connections. Students develop skills in analysis and synthesis.
- From the large-group lectures, students get a more comprehensive view of the whole unit of work before filling in details of the separate parts through independent research and class discussion. They also get a sense of closure from the evaluative summary (Casey, 1964, p. 176).
- An important reason to study at a university is to contact great teachers, to watch and listen to them, and to observe how they approach the topic, the questions they ask, and the research they do. Team teaching enables all students to learn from the best teachers and to enter into conversations between them.
- The teachers model critical thinking for students: They debate, disagree with premises or conclusions, raise new questions, and point out consequences. The contrast of viewpoints encourages more active class participation and independent thinking from students, especially if there is team balance for gender, race, culture, and age. Team teaching is particularly effective with older and underprepared students,

moving beyond communicating facts. Classes arouse their interest and tap into their life experience.

- Today teachers can be at different sites, linked by two-way video, videoconferencing, satellites, or the Internet. Distance learning certainly expands the potential mix of teachers and students.
- Team teaching can also offset the danger of imposing ideas, values, and mind-sets on minorities or less powerful ethnic groups. Teachers of different backgrounds can culturally enrich one another and the students.
- In this context, both students and teachers learn. Listening skills grow. Knowledge is related to life. Schooling is transformed into lifelong learning.
- With so many opportunities to compare techniques, students learn to evaluate themselves, other students, and teachers more accurately.
- Highly motivated students learn more content. They retain more if they can see, hear, or feel what is being taught—or read and write about it or discuss and dramatize and apply it. Team teaching helps both learning and retention by providing more flexibility in the schedule so that students can do more independent study, make better use of library and audiovisual resources, engage in more focused discussion, and plan more creative responses (Arkin, 1996; Wills, 1964).
- Students develop poise in presenting ideas to groups of different sizes. They develop discussion skills from exchanging ideas with more people. These carry over into conversation skills outside the classroom.
- Because several teachers function as a team, term paper assignments, student class presentations, and tests are better spaced instead of being bunched four on one day.
- The presence of more than one teacher reduces student-teacher personality problems. The team approach is perceived as less impersonal and more supportive, breaking down barriers of alienation.
- The presence of more than one teacher makes it possible for the students to be split into small groups for discussion. Active participation—listening and speaking—is encouraged. The students get to know and appreciate one another and the teachers more deeply than in large groups. As a result, most students prefer small groups to large.
- Because both students and teachers learn so well, team teaching boosts student satisfaction. This improves recruitment and retention. Watching the teachers operate as a team encourages the students to form work and social groups. This bonding heightens the self-esteem of all. Having found one another, they want to stay. Others want to join (see LaFauci & Richter, 1970, pp. 65-70, who include several insightful student comments).

On the other hand, team teaching may have some disadvantages for some students:

- Too much variety may hinder habit formation.
- Some students flourish in a highly structured environment that favors repetition.
- Some are confused by conflicting opinions.
- Class preparation is more demanding.

- Class participation requires active involvement rather than mere passive presence.

ADVANTAGES AND DISADVANTAGES FOR ADMINISTRATORS

Advantages of team teaching for administrators are as follows:

- Scheduling can be simplified. Students and teachers are assigned to teams rather than classes.
- Assessment will improve as teachers gain new insights through interaction.
- There will be better use of facilities through improved scheduling of rooms.
- Teachers combine strengths and offset weaknesses. Teaching and learning improve.
- New teachers become oriented more quickly and effectively.
- Teaching teams become a form of in-service training for new and veteran faculty.
- Mutual interaction stimulates research.
- Better learning means happier students and happier faculty—and thus better recruitment and retention of students and faculty.
- The team reduces the adverse impact of teacher absences.
- The presence of more than one teacher reduces student-teacher personality problems.

Team teaching does have some administrative drawbacks:

- Initially, as with any change, time must be invested to reschedule the classrooms to make the maximum potential use of space. And time must be found to discuss the shift to teamwork, with the personality problems and stress that it may bring for the team members. This may not significantly differ from the amount of time administrators already spend with faculty.
- Administrators must also adjust their budgets for foreseeable costs: adequate classroom and media facilities and additional audiovisual and telecommunication materials. They must also consider whether salaries have to be changed to reflect the additional responsibilities undertaken by team members. Team leaders may need some form of bonus. Salary and bonus costs could be met by enlarging some class sizes so that two or more teachers are not doing the work of just one. Administrators could hire nonprofessional staff members to take over some of the nonteaching responsibilities currently carried by faculty: checking attendance, proctoring examinations, showing films and videotapes, monitoring late examinations, collecting and returning papers, grading multiple-choice tests, distributing supplies, helping with classroom housekeeping, assisting with laboratories and field trips, and handling administrative paperwork (Hanslovsky, Moyer, & Wagner, 1969).
- Willingness and ability to team teach is an additional factor to consider in hiring and retention of faculty. It may be more difficult to replace a team member who retires or goes elsewhere.

Section Two

Program Design

3

How to Design a
Team Teaching Program

Even the simplest form of team teaching will profit from some degree of planning. Suppose two teachers with similar class sections of the same course decide to discuss objectives, syllabi, and texts—but to use their own teaching styles and grading norms with their own students. There is already some minimal communication and cooperation but little collaboration. They need not be particularly compatible, but they must be willing to listen and share ideas in order to improve results. Teachers do not need anyone's permission to engage in this minimal form of collaboration. It is still quite informal.

At the other end of the spectrum, a group of several teachers, supported by a full staff of teaching assistants, discuss and agree on all the goals and objectives of a course. They attend one another's lectures to a large group of students, assume responsibility for some of the discussion or research groups constituted from the larger group, apply the same grading system, and meet regularly to fine-tune the process. Compatibility and trust become far more important, along with the ability to give and accept constructive criticism. This more advanced form of team teaching will affect administrative structures, budget, and class schedules, even the entire school.

PRELIMINARIES

Before detailed planning can begin, some preliminary work must be done. The initiative can be taken by the faculty or the administration. Educators have much to learn from industry about giving priority to the search for better ways to reach goals. Much depends on the prevailing culture of the institution—whether it prizes quality and innovation. Because curriculum committees are generally conservative and reluctant to change, the greater the change, the more resistance can be expected. Faculty convocations present opportunities to encourage creative criticism and collaboration. Bit by bit, a climate favoring change will grow (Jones, 1964).

Check the mission and goal statement of the college and any policy statements to determine how compatible they are with team teaching and how team teaching will advance the mission and goals.

See if team teaching has already been used in some departments with success. Its track record in your own school is very important: This will generate resistance or support from influential faculty and administrators.

Study the various factors involved in team teaching. Visit departments or other schools that have used team teaching successfully. Videotapes of what is done in other institutions can trigger new ideas and a variety of options for what might be done in your school. Written critiques sharpen awareness. Consultants may also be useful.

Poll the faculty to determine their interest and willingness to try it. If forced, most will resist. If invited, many will want to try it out.

At this point, move from theory to practice. Decide what subject or subjects will be taught and by whom. Encourage the volunteers to become familiar with the rationale for team teaching. Give them time and opportunity to learn the new skills they shall need.

Foresee any personality problems among the volunteers. Compatibility is essential. If there is any doubt, begin with people who already have similar educational philosophies and communicate with one another well.

Build on this foundation with a preservice orientation workshop, answering questions the teachers have. Focus especially on those arising from trial efforts. Allow ample time for group discussion so that fears and misgivings are voiced and answered. Highlight the improvements to be expected in students and faculty.

Decide on what leadership style the team will find most comfortable and effective: hierarchical or cooperative. If hierarchical, decide how the team leader will be selected. Hidden assumptions about the human dynamics of the team and about what is expected of team members, team leaders, teachers, and students can torpedo the project and frustrate everyone. Chapters 8 through 11 address these issues in detail.

Schedule the time and place for team meetings. At first, the team will need to agree on outcomes and strategies, to develop materials, and to prepare new presentations. All of this will take time.

Determine the clerical help, equipment, rooms, or facilities needed and available.

Start small and grow slowly. Facilities and support are likely to follow an enthusiastic, sincere, and carefully planned beginning (Chamberlin, 1969; see also Davis, 1966).

PLANNING THE TEAM TEACHING PROJECT

Planning to implement team teaching involves the following steps:

1. *Define and prioritize all the essential outcomes.* On the college level, teachers must discuss and settle on the cognitive, affective, and behavioral goals and objectives of the entire program and of each course within the program. What do the team members want the students to know, feel, and do as a result of the program? What information, values, and skills should be learned in each course? What are the students interested in? What do they want to learn? If the team teaching takes place within one department, all the department members should share in these decisions. They will then take ownership of the team-taught courses, and the team will not be perceived as a breakaway group. If the team is interdisciplinary, all the departments concerned should be consulted and kept informed.

2. *Identify and prioritize other desirable but nonessential outcomes.* Chapter 2 discusses many of these from the viewpoint of teachers, students, and administrators. The list given there is not exhaustive. Each program and individual course will have its own particularized goals.

3. *Brainstorm all promising strategies.* Try different ways to look at the course to stimulate creative approaches:

   - Should the general course topic be addressed historically, in terms of past, present, and future? What should be treated first?
   - Will you begin with the easiest or hardest material?
   - Is the sequence determined by thesis, antithesis, synthesis? Can this be changed by feedback from class discussions?
   - Will the arrangement of topics be deductive or inductive, from principle to application or from experience to principle?
   - Should more attention be given to the big picture or to tiny details?
   - If the course is interdisciplinary, are all the pertinent fields represented? Are some essential viewpoints missing? How far should the assumptions, goals, points of view, and methods of each field be explored?
   - Are the contents of each field interconnected as in an ecosystem or juxtaposed like neighbors on a street? If they are interconnected, is the connection organic or mechanical, collaborative or competitive?
   - If the course is like a symphony, will harmony or dissonance be stressed? Is there room for improvisation, as in jazz? How much?

- What can students learn outside class? What learning best takes place in class?
- What methods will be used in each class section: lecture, interruption, discussion, quiz, test, case study, required reading, reflection paper, term paper, dramatization, role playing, field trips, reports, debate, film, tape, videoconferencing? Alternatives should be included to cover emergencies. Study of teaching techniques should be ongoing.
- How will teachers vary the pace and rhythm to keep attention?
- Who will be given priority for released time? On what basis?
- How will classes be covered in case of illness or emergency?

4. *Get the information necessary about factors that would promote or hinder the proposed strategies*:

   - *Environmental factors.* Consider the time of day or year for the course; scheduling policies; classroom size, location, and arrangement; equipment; lighting; sound; and university policies about student behavior, work flow, and records. Some of these issues will be treated in Chapters 4 and 14.
   - *Personality factors.* Build on the strengths of each member of the team. Some team members may prefer to work alone, others to work in groups. Some may like routine work or taking care of details. Some may enjoy the spotlight, others may prefer to work behind the scenes. Some like to lead, others to follow. Will the age, gender, culture, major, abilities, or experience of the students help or impede the attainment of the desired outcomes? How can teachers tap into diversity to enrich the whole group?

5. *Evaluate the proposed strategies.* Weigh them in the light of the essential and desirable outcomes—and of the salient factors mentioned above.

   - Select the strategies that best meet the criteria. Eliminate all proposals that do not meet the necessary conditions. Then drop those that do not meet the desirable goals.
   - Reject strategies that have undesirable side effects. Learn from the mistakes of past team teaching efforts. Foresee and prevent disasters.

6. *Develop an action plan.* Who does what? How? By when? It is important for all members to know what is expected of each team member so that common burdens are fairly shared. The more all agree on goals and means, the less friction will arise.

7. *Plan assessment steps* (see Chapter 12 for details):

   - What information will be needed? How will it be collected? When?
   - Who will make a preliminary evaluation and report to the group? When?
   - Are the school, program, and course learning objectives being met? How well? Why? How are they being monitored?

- How well are the teachers communicating and collaborating?
- Are the teachers' talents and interests being used effectively?
- Is the course on schedule or falling behind? Why?
- Are any students having special problems?

8. *Implement the plan.*

9. *Evaluate the results and redesign the process.* Doing this periodically and regularly promotes creativity, cooperation, and a healthy self-criticism and self-confidence. The team will feel they are pulling together, shoulder to shoulder. Esprit de corps and mutual responsibility grow.

10. *Inform the administration of progress.* Determine in advance what they need to know and when. Their support is crucial in terms of scheduling, equipment, and facilities. They can be quite helpful in foreseeing and resolving personality problems.

11. *Encourage communication within the team.*

- Define clearly and in writing the responsibilities of all team members.
- Provide opportunities for all to express their ideas and needs.
- All team meetings should have a written agenda.
- Written minutes should be kept of all team meetings, including decisions made (Chamberlin, 1969, p. 49).

These principles will not guarantee success, but they will surely reduce the chance of failure.

4

How Best to Serve the Students

STUDENT CHARACTERISTICS AFFECTING LEARNING

Good teaching is student centered. The highest priority in education is helping students to learn. Everything else is chosen to advance that goal: curriculum, administrative staff and structures, faculty personnel and teaching methods, architectural design, and extracurricular activities. This sounds easy but is quite complex. Many factors affecting the students must be taken into account.

Age Level

Older students have more experience and tend to be more critical of the content of lectures. Emotionally more mature, they often are more conscientious about preparing for class through background reading, required or not. Because they are paying for their own education, usually with less financial aid, and sacrificing time away from their family and work, they are making a greater investment and expect a greater return: better lectures and class discussions. Adult learners are often more interested in the why and the how than the what. They want to know the relevance of the material to their lives in the short or long run. They value team teaching highly because this is the way that adults often learn on the job.

Cultural Background

Students from some cultures have been taught that it is disrespectful to question teachers, even if they do not understand what is being said. They consider it insulting to the teacher for them to take notes, as if this implied that the lecture were not clear and memorable. For them, team teaching is invaluable in that it makes clear that it is perfectly acceptable for other teachers to disagree and demand clarification.

Other students have fewer inhibitions and are ready to challenge everything, interrupting lectures constantly, much to the irritation of other students. They can learn from team teaching how to engage in academic discussion while advancing the learning of all involved rather than excessively calling attention to themselves and their own ideas.

Other students want to leap into a conversation without having done the necessary background preparation. For them, classes are times to share ignorance or uninformed opinions. The teachers can model scholarly discourse.

Still others suffer from a kind of cultural arrogance, assuming airs of superiority, as if their own background provided them with the best possible answers to all human questions. They have to learn how to listen with open minds and hearts and be ready to learn from the experience and talents of everyone.

Learning Potential

Not everyone has the same IQ, attention span, ability to deal with abstract concepts, or musical or artistic ability. On a teaching team, it is likely that one of the team members will have rapport with students that other teachers cannot reach effectively. Team teaching has been used with highly selected superior students, highly selected marginal students, and students of relatively limited ability (Chamberlin, 1969, p. 12; Kruger, Struzziero, Watts, & Vacca, 1995; LaFauci & Richter, 1970, p. 2).

Learning Skills

Students must develop the ability to study, read a book, take notes, organize research, and critique arguments. For distance learning, students will need to be able to use computers for e-mail and access to the Internet.

Psychological Readiness

Not all students sitting in a classroom are ready to have their basic assumptions exposed, questioned, even torn apart. They may be insecure for a variety of reasons: childhood and family experiences, previous schooling of a very authoritarian type that tolerated no independent thought, worries about the health of a loved one, the breakup of a romance. They may be plagued by low self-esteem or self-doubt because of former failures. They may be going through personality crises. They may need more attention or counseling than a single teacher is prepared to give.

Motivation

Students in college often take courses to fulfill requirements and resent being there. They would prefer to be anywhere else, doing practically anything else. Teachers have to get their attention and keep it, charm them, and intrigue them with the lure of the subject matter so that their appetite is whetted. A teaching team at least provokes them to ask why intelligent people want to study this area. The number of teachers multiplies the likelihood of addressing the genuine needs and interests of these students.

Attitudes

Attitudes can be affected by all kinds of things: moods of boredom or hyper-activity, psychological blocks or prejudices, distractions from outside noises, the weather, the time of day, health, physical fatigue, hunger, disabilities, fear of computers, or pressures from peers, parents, or jobs. The presence of more than one teacher heightens the likelihood of coping effectively with these interior and exterior obstacles to learning.

TEAM TEACHING OF LARGE GROUPS

Team teaching can address many of the above issues by varying class sizes. Sharing information can be done readily in large groups in a lecture, debate, or panel format. Films, class demonstrations, videos, educational television, and quizzes and tests can all be given to very large assemblies quite efficiently by in-dividual teachers because the content is fixed ahead of time.

Teachers tend to prepare much more thoroughly for presentations before a large group, especially if the audience will contain some interested colleagues. They may use overhead projectors, slides, videos, chalkboards, and computer graphics, appealing to sight as well as sound. The pace may be brisk, but repetition can be easily built in to reinforce the most important content (Davis, 1966, pp. 44-48).

Team teaching also draws from a larger pool of expertise and teaching styles. Teachers teach one another along with the students. Opportunities for growth abound. Teachers may develop new texts or videos. For example, the Open University in Britain has teams of teachers design video modules for use in class at different sites.

Lectures can provide basic orientation, motivation, and enrichment. Because of a tightly knit, orderly arrangement of ideas, much content can be presented in a short time. Teachers may highlight interrelationships between subject areas or applications of ideas to life. Good lectures may use real objects, demonstrations, and film clips to appeal to the imagination, pique curiosity, and stimulate research. Students can also learn how to take notes and outline the lecture. Their awareness of the structure will help them to organize their own ideas. Because this is so important, teachers should periodically check students' skills in note taking and outlining.

All of this would be true even outside a context of team teaching. In some colleges, therefore, presentations to very large numbers of students are given by only one member of the team, the one best qualified to give that lecture. In such a situation, the students know what to expect: a lecture, film, or test. They are mentally prepared to listen. They readily pay attention. The other teachers may or may not attend.

Lectures, however, often become more lively if given by more than one instructor. Instead of allowing students to remain passive, the team can interrupt one another, appeal to student experiences to validate or question assumptions, and generally model scholarly discussion, inviting students to enter actively, even aggressively, into the conversation. They can challenge the accuracy and relevance of the students' notes. In such a situation, the lecture content cannot remain fixed. The teachers adapt to one another and the students, even students at a distance, when simultaneous two-way video is used.

The primary goal of the lecture shifts away from giving information to engaging higher-order intellectual skills. Learning the facts is left to research—reading articles and books or materials downloaded from the Internet. Class time is used for more important issues, like sifting through the abundance of facts to question their validity, reliability, and relevance.

A Socratic method of questioning moves the audience from a passive to active stance, encouraging independent thought—but it can be very time consuming. On the other hand, teachers find it easier to ask leading questions in large rather than small groups because excellent questioning skills are beyond the scope of student discussion leaders (Hyman, 1970, p. 77). Large groups should have an opportunity for discussion during or after a lecture. But care must be taken lest only a few students want to ask or answer all the questions.

Promptness is essential for large classes. Latecomers inconvenience the entire group.

TEAM TEACHING OF SMALL GROUPS

After the general presentation or testing on material, split large groups into smaller units, with each team member assuming leadership for a small group or seminar. This will require the availability of smaller-sized rooms, one per group. With good scheduling, large lecture halls can be used for different classes, so that students in Course A meet on Monday in Lecture Hall A and on Wednesday in Classrooms W, X, Y, and Z and students in Course B meet on Monday in Classrooms W, X, Y, and Z and on Wednesday in Lecture Hall A. Alternatively, a large area with movable chairs and proper acoustics can allow several small groups to go on at the same time, much like conversations at different tables in a restaurant. The noise level rarely bothers the students.

Discussions, case studies, debates, panels, and sharing experiences are much more effective in small groups. Attention shifts from the visual to the auditory, though simulation games, dramatization, and role playing appeal to both. Here the students are more actively engaged in the formation of the critical skills of analysis, evaluation, and synthesis. Here, too, the emotional dimensions of issues are not only felt but explicitly explored. Habits of respect for the material being studied as well as for the dignity and talents of all present are built up. Students here learn how to learn from from team members and from one another. In this way, one can tap into the rich resources of a multicultural, even multilingual group of students and teachers. A sense of community is enhanced. This context promotes an inductive approach to learning, encouraging reflection on experience, which leads to discovery and greater appreciation.

Discussion gives students an opportunity to clarify their thinking by talking their ideas through, checking how accurately they understood the lectures, getting feedback about aspects they did not notice, foregrounding assumptions that they took for granted, considering consequences they did not foresee. In the process, they improve brainstorming and communication skills, engage in problem solving, and strengthen interpersonal relations. Peer pressure usually guarantees serious participation, especially where students are paying their own tuition. Students readily recognize and praise solid contributions, and this encourages all to do their best.

Teachers who are present can assess the students' grasp of the course content and discover areas that need clarification. They can note positive or negative attitudes to the subject and the abilities of individual students to handle data and analyze problems. The teachers can evaluate the effectiveness of their own teaching and learn how to improve or correct their large-group presentations.

For all this to happen, teachers on a team must develop their skills in conducting fruitful discussions: devising intriguing questions, having the students answer one another's questions rather than waiting for the teachers to provide answers, and preventing a few articulate students from dominating the conversation of the rest. Teachers must establish a learning environment where all feel comfortable in sharing and critiquing ideas with openness and respect.

If more than one team member can be present, team teaching is even more provocative within a small group, more easily drawing all group members into participation. One team member can assume leadership of the small group, focusing on content; the other may concentrate on the process, making sure no one is overlooked, reinforcing minority viewpoints, and filling in gaps.

More usually, the team members go from one small group to another, ensuring that the discussion or dramatization goes well, then moving on. In this case, students appointed by the teachers or elected by the group assume leadership of each group.

Student leaders should get some training on how to maintain order politely, involving all in the discussion, allowing minority viewpoints to be heard, sticking to the topic, and staying within the allotted time. The teaching team should provide the student teaching assistants with a set of stimulating questions based on the large-group presentation.

A student other than the leader can act as recorder, preparing a summary orally or in writing, so that the teachers can guage progress and learn what topics need further development.

Another student can function as observer, focusing on the process rather than on the content, noticing what questions were fruitful and why, how successfully all were drawn into active participation, and how comments were received. Still another student can note connections between subject areas and point out salient applications to life.

Rotating responsibilities within the small group enables many students to develop hidden talents and to appreciate the abilities of others. This encourages student interaction, builds community, and stimulates learning.

How should students be assigned to such discussion groups? Teachers can try different approaches. One teacher may prefer a cross section of age, culture, and proficiency in each group. Others may prefer more homogeneity. Others may wish to rotate group membership at regular intervals. Much depends on the outcomes desired from the discussions: interest, mutual appreciation, course information, student skills. Members of a teaching team usually want several learning outcomes.

Team teaching puts much emphasis on active student participation and small-group processes. To forestall problems that some students might experience with this, some colleges have found it helpful to provide materials at registration time, describing what to expect in such courses. Students then can ask others with more experience what this is like in practice. During the semester, judicious use of office hours for counseling, coupled with informal faculty-student get-togethers outside class, can set a tone of mutual collaboration and respect (LaFauci & Richter, 1970, pp. 63-65).

TEAM TEACHING OUTSIDE THE CLASSROOM

Outside the classroom, much can be left to student initiative: research in the library, on the Internet, in the field, in language or science laboratories, or using computer-assisted and programmed instruction. The teaching team may want to encourage the students to use e-mail or to meet personally to work together on team projects, research, and reports, written or oral, modeled on the behavior of the teachers themselves.[1]

This prepares them well for much career work in the military, business, artistic, and academic worlds. The ultimate goal of education is to teach students how to learn so that they can continue to grow throughout life.

Field trips can be large-group activities easily combined with small-group interaction. Much will depend on what is readily available in the locality: museums, concerts, opera, religious and civic festivals, parks, beaches, historical sites, wildlife sanctuaries. Information can be gathered while social skills grow. The teaching team must prepare the students ahead of time, alerting them to what to look for and how to make written reports.

DISCIPLINE

Sources of Disciplinary Problems

Discipline is a factor often overlooked in planning, carrying out, and evaluating team teaching. Several sources of disciplinary problems may be noted, including those noted here.

Conflicting Goals of School, Teachers, and Students

The university's mission statement usually sets forth the results it expects from students who attend: its cognitive, affective, and behavioral objectives—what it wants the students to know, feel, and do. A liberal education should be genuinely liberating from unexamined assumptions and pressures. It should also familiarize students with a culture or subculture and its norms and values.

The teachers who make up the team may agree or disagree with those goals and may rank them very differently than the university board of trustees, administration, or even the faculty as a whole. They may disagree among themselves about what they want the students to learn: information about important facts, certain skills of the discipline, critical thinking, or self-expression.

The students may have altogether different goals: to get out of college or this course with as little work and as high a grade as possible, to get a job, to make friends, to discover their own identity, or to satisfy curiosity. Some students reject whatever they think an institution or society wants to impose on them. Some are liberal, others conservative.

Group Influence

Students live in overlapping groups—teams, gangs, clubs, and cliques that may be determined by age, interests, current fashion in clothes, music, politics, and/or family and cultural background. These groups may have conflicting expectations about what is important to learn and how to learn it. Some groups encourage open self-expression and active participation in class discussions and activities; other groups inhibit it. Some encourage a clash of ideas; others suppress it. Some encourage self-control; others exert group pressure. Work, social, and sexual relationships and status within the group often shift among group members. The teachers must be aware of the many dimensions of group dynamics and remain flexible. Wherever possible, the teaching team should decide how to enlist the individuals and their groups to reinforce the goals and objectives of the class.

Individual Differences

Students have different needs, interests, motivations, and moods. They have developed different communication skills. Some seek attention by overachieving, others by underachieving, some by speaking up, others by keeping silent. One great advantage of team teaching is that different students will be attracted by the different personalities of the teachers. These natural attractions can be taken advantage of to draw out the shy and inarticulate students, engaging them more fully in the learning process inside and outside of class.

Personal Problems

Teachers are growing more sensitive to learning problems such as dyslexia, attention deficit disorder, and hearing difficulties. Inadequate diet, psychological or physical abuse, or too little sleep may seem beyond the ability of teachers to repair, but good teachers should be alert to signs of these situations so that they can talk to students about them personally or send them to skilled counselors.

Disciplinary Coping Techniques

Self-control and self-direction are skills that are developed slowly, with much encouragement. Teachers can help by highlighting and building on the values of the groups to which the students belong. Their own enthusiasm for the subject can be catching. They can learn by experience to foresee and sidestep dangerous situations. By skilled questioning, they can get and keep attention. By judicious use of visual aids, they can cut down on distractions. By careful planning of every minute of class time, and by varying activities because of the limited attention span of students, they can prevent boredom and restlessness. The teaching team's courteous treatment of one another and of the students models the kind of behavior they want.

Discuss with the students the reasons underlying class expectations—why everyone must be able to repeat and rephrase a student's statement or question before discussing an answer, why formal papers must meet a higher standard of spelling and grammar than informal essays, why everyone must do the background reading before class. Students give teachers the benefit of the doubt, but they also expect teachers to be reasonable and consistent. Teachers on a team can periodically review as a group how they are forestalling and handling disciplinary problems. Different team members can assume responsibility to contact difficult students and work out remedies.

Surprisingly, discipline problems become much less in a large group. This may be due to the presence of more than one teacher in the room. Or the students may be influenced by a certain "mind-set." They quickly learn what kind of behavior is expected in lecture halls. They readily give attention and are less easily distracted (Davis, 1966; Tomchek, 1964).

NOTE

1. *Syllabus, Technological Horizons in Education,* and *Imaging* frequently have useful articles on teaching in the Information Age.

Who Picks the Team and How

SELECTING THE TEAM

Administrators, faculty, and students all have legitimate concerns about the selection of teachers to form the team.

Administrators worry about budget, faculty workload, and instructional quality. Will faculty with a full-time load simply take on the additional stress of preparing to teach with colleagues? Will they expect their teaching load to be decreased? If so, who will replace or help them?

Will class size be doubled or tripled or more, depending on how many faculty are on the team? What will be the largest class? If class sizes remain the same but some form of distance learning takes place through closed-circuit television or multiple videos, will the teachers simply remain with their classes, or will aides replace them?

Will only the best teachers be selected to form teams? Why bother, if they are already successful? Are the improvements from team teaching so spectacular that they justify all the administrative burdens of finding space, adjusting schedules, and paying for the changes?

On the other hand, can relatively poor teachers be improved by teaming them with others who will serve as mentors? Or will their dead weight drag down otherwise exciting and enthusiastic teachers?

Will the faculty be chosen from a pool of volunteers? Can anyone volunteer? What criteria will be used to select the teams? Can faculty simply be assigned, regardless of how they feel about teaching on a team? Will team members be from the same or different disciplines? Will the faculty not on teams become jealous or resentful?

How will these decisions be reached? How much authority can and should be delegated? Will all those affected by the decisions be involved in arriving at the decisions? Who should make the final decision? In what manner should the assignments be made? Unilaterally by administrators? By majority vote of the faculty? By consensus? Will students have any voice in the process?

Will the teachers on each team have a balance of age, gender, ethnic background, and/or experience (Havas, 1994)? Will innovative and traditional teachers be mixed? Will team members be rotated periodically? Will each team have a single leader or a master teacher, or will leadership be shared?

How will course content be determined? By the teaching team? By the departments? By a curriculum committee of the college? By national or regional professional accrediting associations? By administrators, taking into account the mission and goals statements of the college and department?

Who will evaluate the team? The students, using standardized forms? Team members? Departments, using criteria agreed upon beforehand? Administrators?

There are arguments for and against all sides of the above issues. Thorough discussion beforehand can prevent bruised feelings and improve the chances for success.

Answers to these questions will differ according to the spirit and culture of each university. Some organizations move from the top down, others from the bottom up. Some prefer tight control; others encourage individual or team autonomy as far as possible. Where will lines be drawn? Ill feeling and problems can be forestalled if all who are affected by a decision are involved in making the decision. But insisting on consensus can be a way to avoid any change, no matter how valuable. Minorities can be tyrannical—but majorities can also be unreasonable.

Frequent two-way communication between administration and faculty becomes even more important. More of the communication content must focus on reasons that will affect decisions rather than information about decisions already made.

Communication within the team must also be open and frequent. Conflict about who is in control, about who has responsibility to do what, and about the best ways to present content and evaluate progress must be resolved. Otherwise, the students become guinea pigs in a badly planned experiment.

Trust among faculty members and between the faculty and administration is needed for such educational innovations to work. Mutual respect is undercut by gossip and pettiness.

It should be relatively easy to get students' approval: They can be counted on to welcome any sort of change, provided it will be evaluated for effectiveness.

Accountability is a key issue. As far as possible, responsibilities of each team member should be specified:

- Attendance at team planning and class sessions
- Role in class presentations
- Asking and answering questions of students and faculty
- Design, administration, and grading of tests
- Reading and grading papers
- Student advising and supervision
- Selection of required and recommended texts and audiovisual materials
- Use of guest speakers

Administrators usually appoint, promote, and terminate faculty with varying levels of input from departments and students. How will the teams be involved in the process? Will they actually make the decision, merely be consulted, or not be consulted at all?

In choosing new teachers, attention should be given to their potential for team teaching. They may be asked about their attitude toward this and may demonstrate their skills as part of the interview process. Candidates inexperienced with teamwork should observe some classes and learn the responsibilities of teammates, discussing with team members the pros and cons of team teaching. The team can then assess the candidate's attitudes, interests, and ability to function as a team member.

Internship programs in interdisciplinary team teaching afford opportunities for junior faculty to participate in curriculum development, supervised class presentations in several different disciplines, and observation of a variety of excellent teaching methods used by the best professors in the college. The newcomers can start slowly, then gradually assume more responsibilities in a supportive context with steady feedback.

Once a teacher is appointed, colleagues on a team often know more about a person's strengths and weaknesses than do other members of that person's department because of firsthand observation. They have many opportunities to provide mentoring advice and support. They may also provide valuable letters of recommendation for promotion and tenure.

Team teaching presents excellent opportunities for in-service education of faculty. Work on the team stimulates members to define goals clearly, weigh the effectiveness of means to reach the goals, and test the results. As members discuss these issues, they are more likely to keep abreast of research in education as well as in their fields of expertise. The students stand to benefit from this.

PREREQUISITES

Attention should be paid to the special dynamics characteristic of small groups. The frequent interaction brings benefits but also potential friction. Some ground rules should be agreed upon to eliminate possible friction among teammates:

- All teachers should feel free to preserve their own individual classroom styles. No one should be pressured to adopt different techniques and traits that work effectively for others. One strength of a team is that the different teachers complement, rather than mimicking, one another.
- On the other hand, teachers should also feel free to try out something new and get some feedback on how it works.
- Compatibility is another major concern. Team members need not all be friends; indeed, the stresses of the team may strain previous friendships. But they must be willing to listen to others' ideas, to give and receive suggestions for improvement, and to subordinate personal independence to the good of the group. Some teachers may be too shy or introverted. Some may not want to change their own personal and effective approach. If some members worry about betrayal by others or if some feel that they are not respected because of age, gender, or cultural background, genuine teamwork becomes very difficult to achieve.
- Team meetings should begin and end on time and follow an agenda prepared ahead of time, to ensure punctual and faithful attendance. This sets a businesslike tone and prevents resentment at tardiness and absenteeism.
- When teams do not have teaching assistants, team members should agree to pick up the slack and do what aides might do elsewhere (Hanslovsky et al., 1969).

As Heller (1964) has commented,

Ideally, team teachers would be the epitome of intellectual, professional, and personal virtue. Actually, the qualifications of effective team teachers are not so demanding. In fact the same qualities which make teachers effective in a conventional setting make them effective in a team teaching situation. (p. 146)

The team nurtures intelligence, enthusiasm, curiosity, patience, and imagination, qualities needed in any teacher. But it is particularly supportive of individual talents. With practice, one member may become an excellent lecturer for large groups, developing dynamic presentations, humor, and a good theatrical sense. Another may become an expert in guiding student-centered discussions with effective group dynamics. Still another may be most skillful in inspiring students to initiate projects, do research, and write creatively (Heller, 1964).

Whatever the type of team—hierarchical, democratic, or mixed—to be successful, the team members must

- Be willing to work hard, giving time and energy. Planning takes time. Coordination of lesson plans—and personalities—takes time. Evaluation and redesign take time. Results are proportionate to efforts expended. Each member should bear a fair share of the load. If outside responsibilities prevent a teacher from functioning as a team member, something has to give. The team can help the troubled member to clarify the values involved and come to a reasonable solution acceptable to all.

- Be genuinely interested in students' educational development. Granted that experience on the team can stimulate interest in the topics and spark creative research in the faculty, the main reason for team teaching is to improve the quality and quantity of student learning. This must be the main focus in evaluation.
- Be willing to share good ideas with colleagues. Pooling insights and techniques is mutually enriching. Everyone's teaching can improve as colleagues listen to one another teach and evaluate the results. Star teachers, no matter how famous, can be helped by specialists in particular subjects, by generalists skilled in seeing interrelationships with other topics, by media and technology types, by experts in group dynamics, and by communication experts who focus on the teaching process. Even opera singers have voice coaches. Actors have directors (Esterby-Smith, 1984).
- Be willing to give, receive, and use constructive criticism. For this, a strong personal sense of security is essential. Many faculty fear bruising the feelings or hampering the academic freedom of others. Rightly so. There must be mutual respect. But concern for the common good demands serious self-criticism and criticism of the whole team effort to achieve the agreed-upon goals of the course. A climate must be established where team members feel free to question, disagree, or express delight. Honest discussions of doubts and fears along with excitement and enthusiasm will improve the caliber of the teaching of all faculty members. Once this atmosphere is established, it must be periodically renewed to keep communication channels open.
- Be willing to cooperate and solve problems together. Team members should be committed to a group process of decision making. Creativity and resilience are essential to this process. They readily appear in brainstorming sessions. Teammates should be neither domineering nor easily squelched, but ready to compete, compromise, and collaborate. They should willingly accept and fulfill the responsibilities assigned to them. And getting feedback from colleagues can be quite encouraging, but only if all are open and flexible.
- Recognize that some ideas and teaching techniques work better than others. Just because some ways of presenting material work does not mean that other approaches might not work better. All of this is being done for the sake of the students. Students respond differently to different types of presentations for many reasons.
- Be willing to take risks and learn from mistakes. Experimenting within the framework of the team can be very fruitful precisely because several heads are better than one and risks of failure are cut (Johnson & Hunt, 1968, p. 21).

GETTING STARTED

When team teaching is just getting off the ground at a school, it is easiest to begin with two sections of one course or one discipline. Once the team members get used to teamwork, they may invite members from other departments and become interdisciplinary (Beggs, 1964a).

A well-designed orientation program, combining theory and practice, can be most helpful to teachers. It should cover the objectives, advantages, and pitfalls of team teaching; the different roles and responsibilities of team members; successful methods for large- and small-group work; and the opportunities for teacher and student creativity and growth.

The first task is to determine the learning outcomes that are desired. For this, the entire department may get involved so that they all feel ownership of the project.

Next, discuss and select the best means to achieve those goals: the choice of required and recommended texts, the frequency and content of lectures, audiovisuals, discussions, and individual research.

The team must then decide on the optimal group size for the lectures and discussions, taking into account the limitations of the rooms available to the team and the number of teachers who are teammates.

Assignment of students to discussion groups is also decided by the team. Teachers may sometimes want a certain homogeneity in the student group so that they can explore an issue in depth. Other times, they want diversity in the group to expose the students to a breadth of viewpoints.

Consider how much time will be devoted to formal presentations, how much to discussions or laboratory work. Development of certain skills calls for more frequent meetings to assess progress and reinforce the learning.

Finally, the team should discuss how testing and grading may best be done to promote as much learning as possible:

- Well-constructed multiple-choice tests can give a clear view of what information students have mastered. Teachers also can assess the development of certain skills by looking at the results. Such tests take a long time to compose but can be rapidly corrected.
- Essays give a more accurate picture of students' ability to analyze and synthesize, to see connections and draw conclusions, and to express themselves in writing. They tap into the students' imagination, creativity, and emotion more effectively than multiple-choice tests.
- Oral skills can be observed in group discussions, but the team may want to schedule some oral examinations also, either with individuals or with very small groups.
- Scores of students on Graduate Record Examinations, Law School Aptitude Tests, Nursing State Board Examinations, and Bar Examinations all give some objective insight into what progress has been made. Of course, many other factors also affect students' scores. But consistent improvement of performance in competition with other students is very encouraging for students and teachers alike.

Types of Teams

Team teaching may be done in *authority-directed (hierarchical)* teams, *self-directed (democratic, synergetic)* teams, or *coordinated or mixed (hierarchical/democratic)* teams. (For more details, including charts, see Davis, 1966; LaFauci & Richter, 1970.)

AUTHORITY-DIRECTED TEAMS

In authority-directed or hierarchical teams, members and leaders are assigned by department chairs (if the team is intradisciplinary) or deans (if the team is interdisciplinary). The team has a leader, who is helped by master teachers, regular teachers, and sometimes interns or aides.

The leader or executive is in charge of the team, much like a department chair. He or she

- Chairs meetings
- Schedules, coordinates, and directs team activities
- Makes specified decisions on behalf of the team
- Stimulates thought and action about goals and methods
- Keeps abreast of pertinent literature
- Encourages and implements research
- Contacts community resource persons
- Acts as a role model, particularly in teaching and testing
- Orients and assists teachers, especially newcomers
- Trains and supervises interns and aides
- Appraises progress
- Maintains records
- Communicates information to and from the team

- Acts as a general resource person
- Integrates the team program with other programs
- Teaches, especially large groups and introductory units
- Receives a higher salary or release time

The master teacher or senior teacher

- Regularly teaches large-group classes, sometimes small
- Develops curricular resources for a special subject area
- Keeps up to date on professional literature for that area
- Acts as a resource person for that area for other teachers
- Gives planning leadership for that area
- Advises the team leader of special team needs
- Acts as a role model, stimulating thought and action (Chamberlin, 1969; Hanslovsky et al., 1969)

The regular team teacher

- Shares planning about content and methods
- Studies student records to determine special needs
- Teaches groups of various sizes
- Leads discussions in small groups, clarifying ideas, helping students think, question, and discuss, and ensuring mutual listening and respect
- Supervises the work of interns and aides

The teaching assistant, aide, or intern

- Participates actively in team meetings
- Monitors groups jointly watching videos or a lecture given via closed-circuit television
- Shows films
- Works with students in large and small groups and individually
- Leads discussions
- Develops bibliographies and does library research
- Prepares instructional materials, including visual aids
- Duplicates and distributes instructional materials
- Explains purpose and details of instructional materials
- Guides practice to achieve mastery of content and skills
- Stimulates student interest and development
- Checks attendance
- Types examinations
- Proctors and grades objective tests
- Corrects essays for spelling and grammar
- Secures, prepares, and shows films and videotapes
- Collects and returns papers

- Distributes supplies
- Helps with classroom housekeeping
- Maintains a program bulletin board
- Assists with laboratories and field trips
- Runs study halls
- Handles administrative paperwork.

Performance of these tasks by interns or aides frees time for the leaders and other team teachers to engage in planning, research, and other more advanced tasks.

Hierarchical teaching teams periodically give common examinations to their students to test their progress and proficiency in learning the desired knowledge, attitudes, values, and skills. Students are expected to grasp concepts, master facts, and articulate ideas logically and systematically. The teachers are assumed to know best what and how the students should learn. Emphasis is on fulfilling the course requirements, especially cognitive content.

This approach allows small groups of faculty to handle large groups of students, with or without the use of teaching assistants. This saves money. If paraprofessional aides are hired, this may increase the costs somewhat, but many nonteaching tasks may be delegated to them, as mentioned above. The overall quality of instruction rises.

The hierarchical structure has several advantages. Decisions can be made fairly rapidly, without endless debate. Direction can be provided, duties clearly specified, responsibilities assumed. But some members may resent not having decision-making power.

SELF-DIRECTED TEAMS

Self-directed, autonomous, or synergetic teams are spontaneously formed by faculty and/or students. All the teachers are considered equal. Decisions are usually made by consensus or by majority vote. Control is not a major issue. But endless discussions can be frustrating.

If the administration demands a leader, teammates may rotate the leadership periodically or according to the expertise needed. The leader does not get extra pay or time off. Teaching aides are not normally hired.

These teams usually vary in size and function according to faculty interests, talents, and goals. Often they give students a role in selecting the topics to be studied. Because students learn by doing, research is expected, done either individually or in teams. Personal relations among students and between students and faculty are encouraged to facilitate collaborative learning.

Informality and creativity are prized. Emphasis is on growth in many dimensions of the personality rather than merely on linear mastery of information. No examinations or grades need be given, though this may be done to meet graduation or transfer requirements.

COORDINATED TEAMS

Coordinated teams combine elements of the two preceding types. Members are appointed by administrators after consultation with the faculty on their interests and preferences. Team members typically are drawn from several departments that share a core curriculum. Teams may select and often rotate their own coordinators or leaders. Such decisions are best based on the coordinator's experience, leadership qualities, and enthusiasm for team teaching.

Not all teachers want to be team leaders. Many are quite content to exercise their leadership with students and want to save their energies for that. But teaching teams provide a context for various leadership qualities to emerge and be recognized. And the rest of the team profit from the enthusiasm, vision, and thoughtfulness of the leaders.

Innovations are encouraged, and modifications in class size and time are permitted, whatever works best. Faculty evaluate students on their achievement of the learning goals; students evaluate faculty on their proficiency. Emphasis is on student and faculty growth within the context of the learning goals of the course. There is a balance between initiative and shared responsibility, between democratic participation and common expectations, between student development and the clear and interesting presentation of content, and between cognitive, affective, and behavioral outcomes.

Differentiated responsibilities, along with clear job descriptions, provide opportunities for senior faculty to share their expertise with junior members, for the recognition of special teaching or counseling talents, and for the provision of prestige along with certain titles, perhaps even special compensation. Salary might be adjusted according to the quantity and quality of work done, as long as all receive pay comparable to that of other teachers of the same rank.

"Team teaching is an extension of the concept of increased quality performance through cooperative specialization" (Beggs, 1964a, p. 44). As in industry and many professions, specialization in teaching improves the quality of the end product: student learning. But unlike manufacturing, education is not aimed at achieving standardization but at heightening adaptation to the individual needs of the students and to the talents of the teachers.

Some teachers can specialize in selecting learning experiences, others in lecturing, others in leading class discussions, still others in designing tests. All can help one another. Doing what one does best provides satisfaction, which is often worth more than money.

For coordinated teams to work, preplanning is essential. Members and leaders should be selected a year ahead, ensuring some continuation in membership and projects. All members should do some preliminary research so that they know what to expect from team teaching. This may include both reading and talking with members of already existing teams and perhaps visiting them on site to watch them in action. In this way, many worries are dispelled.

Dreaming and brainstorming about the possibilities of this teaching method can get hopes and fears out in the open. Then they can be confronted before detailed planning begins. Less competent teachers tend to be reluctant to expose their intellectual or professional weaknesses. They need to be reassured of the respect and support of other team members.

Goals, materials, and schedules can be settled in team meetings. Students may be invited to express their concerns. Needs of the academic program can be coordinated with the personality and preferences of team members. Mixing junior and senior faculty, male and female faculty, and faculty of different ethnic backgrounds and with varied attitudes toward teaching the course content makes for lively class discussions. It also ensures respect for academic freedom. Disruptive clash of personalities should be avoided, but disagreements on means to an end keep everyone awake.

Continuity may be ensured if at least some members of the team stay with the project for several years. New members will be added because of normal attrition or changing interests of the faculty. Personality clashes may start up or grow. Although cliques should be avoided, faculty requests for assignment or transfer should be honored as much as possible. This guarantees that team members are there because they want to be. Their rapport makes creative work and desirable results more likely.

Team leaders may receive extra pay because of their added responsibilities. Or administrators may grant release time to an entire team to work on a special project, such as developing a research proposal, designing a new curriculum, or opening up a whole new area for team teaching.

In colleges where several such coordinated teams operate, the team coordinators or leaders may form a council to share ideas and concerns with one another and the administration. They may invite students to attend and participate in planning.

Fields of Team Teaching

To become proficient in a discipline, students should learn the key organizing concepts of the field, master the most significant facts in that area, and see the relationships between the various subjects. Team teaching, whether within one subject field or cutting across several, attempts to balance the need for teachers and students to specialize with the opportunity to broaden horizons. Teachers are expected to do research and publication in depth to achieve mastery within a field. Usually this demands narrowing one's focus to an area that can be thoroughly understood. Students, too, attempt to understand a whole by breaking it down into parts. But overemphasis on analysis of smaller and smaller units of reality endangers both teachers and students. Researchers may lose sight of important implications and applications of their work. One-sided approaches give skewed results. The solution: synthesis, putting the pieces back together again, imaginatively asking new questions and discovering new relationships. Students are alerted to the complexity of real-life situations and problems.

How is this done?

> Two or more teachers, with or without teacher aides, cooperatively plan, instruct and evaluate one or more class groups in an appropriate instructional space and given length of time, so as to take advantage of the special competencies of the team members. (Singer, 1964, p.16)

This can be done within one discipline or across disciplines.

SINGLE-DISCIPLINARY TEAMS

A single-discipline team consists of teachers from the same department teaching a common set of students. Team members may or may not have the same specialty within the field, but they usually bring different research interests.

Team teaching within a department is a relatively simple way to get experience with the dynamics of a team, for many department members already know and trust one another and may be curious about how others approach the material. There is less fear of public humiliation when the limits of their knowledge are revealed. In fact, they can rely on one another to keep the pace of class lively and to supplement data with stories. Just the variety of voices and personalities stimulates interest.

Team teaching within a discipline exposes a teacher's specific talents to at least twice as many students as in a conventional schedule. It permits a new teacher to work with a veteran in an in-service program. Team members can practice continuous curriculum planning and revision, based on student needs as well as their own assets and interests. They may bring in community resource specialists or use films, tapes, closed-circuit television, self-instruction programs, and other technological learning tools.

The department usually takes overall responsibility for the course objectives—cognitive, behavioral, and affective. These include knowledge of the basic facts together with in-depth familiarity or even mastery of certain areas; skills of analysis, synthesis, and critical judgment; and certain attitudes and values characteristic of the field. If departments exercise this degree of supervision of all the courses, it is a relatively simple step to move to team teaching.

Department members together set the course goals and content, select common materials such as texts and films, and develop tests and final examinations to be given to all students. Within these parameters, team members set the sequence of topics and supplemental materials. They also give their own interpretations of the materials and use their own teaching styles. The greater the agreement on common objectives and interests, the more likely that teaching will be interdependent and coordinated.

This approach is comparatively easy to administer and find rooms for, especially if several different teams take turns using the large classrooms.

Teaching periods can be scheduled side by side or consecutively. For example, teachers of two similar classes may team up during the same or adjacent periods so that the teachers can focus on that phase of the course that each can best handle. Students can meet sometimes all together, sometimes in small groups supervised by individual teachers or teaching assistants; or they can work singly or together on projects in the library, the laboratory, or the field.

Where all students belong to the same department, class discussions should be able to focus more often on issues of common interest. Students from the same department will also be more likely to share other classes, know one another, and interact more frequently and informally outside the common class. Students from the same department feel freer to bring up what they consider to be conflicts between their own discipline and another without worrying whether they are wasting the time of students from other departments.

INTERDISCIPLINARY TEAMS

The interdisciplinary team has teachers from different departments using a common block of time to instruct a common set of students, often within the general education core curriculum. Within the set time frame, classes can be broken into large or small groups of varying sizes, down to individual study. Teachers can plan how to divide the block into daily, weekly, or monthly chunks. They may lecture, lead discussion, field questions, or supervise research or tutorials. Joint planning and evaluation can be built into the schedule.

After a long period of ever-narrowing specialization, university faculty have expressed interest in problems that range across subject area and even college lines. Nursing professors, for example, are understandably interested in health sciences, but also in psychology, sociology, politics, history, business, law, and ethics. All of these fields have immediate impact on the availability and quality of nursing care.

Another example: Broadening appreciation of a biblical text can come through study of the various meanings of the words used in their original language; of the meanings of those words at different historical epochs; of their use in different situations according to gender, social standing, and cultural assumptions; of citations of the text by other biblical authors; of literary use of the text in translations by writers of other cultures; of interpretations of the text by commentators of different theological traditions over the centuries; and of the different purposes and uses of language in general. Philology, history, sociology, psychology, anthropology, literature, and communication arts all provide useful insights into what the text meant for its original audience—and what it has meant for other audiences since. Exclusive use of only one approach impoverishes scholarship—and religion.

A great advantage of interdisciplinary team teaching is demonstrating the relationships between the subject areas studied, opening both teachers and students to new points of view, new questions, and new discoveries. One of the exciting offshoots is joint research projects about problems that surface in class. By suggesting topics, students have direct input in shaping their curriculum. These projects can vary in length and depth from assignments to two or more students for a class presentation or paper to long-term research jointly done by the faculty (and even students) and resulting in scholarly publications.

Another benefit of such multifaceted problem-oriented teaching is that it connects learning with real life—which is messy and complex, with many viewpoints and alternative solutions. Prior learning is applied to new situations, reinforced, and stretched. Similarities and differences emerge. Skills develop. Interests grow. A course on the city, for example, calls for expertise in history, economics, politics, sociology, ethics, communication arts, architecture, and engineering.

On the other hand, because several departments are involved, more planning and coordination are required. More people will have to put in more time. More attention will have to be paid to the possibilities of clashing personalities. Where conflict arises, this can be creative. It can also be destructive. Techniques of conflict resolution must be learned.[1]

Exploration and resolution of false conflicts between disciplines should significantly improve students' attitudes toward them. Such conflicts now often go undiscussed in many classes and breed doubts. Classes in which the content is interdisciplinary and related to the student's major will have a greater impact. Such a class builds on already existing interests and deliberately tries to integrate the subject with life.

Classes that are team taught will have even more impact, and the effect will be still higher if the team is interdisciplinary, with one of the members related to the students' major. Team teaching usually involves a variety of approaches to a subject area, thus stimulating interest. Different role models are offered for imitation that complement one another and appeal to different types of students. Several teachers who share the same attitudes and values, critically arrived at, heighten the plausible importance of those values.

In the interdisciplinary approach to team teaching, curriculum provides the loom upon which different disciplines using different colored thread weave their kaleidoscope of color into a tapestry (see Hanslovsky et al., 1969, for several examples). For example, in an interdisciplinary course taught by professors of communication arts, physics, mathematics, and psychology, each could focus on the importance of sensation and the senses; the importance of light and darkness, camera angle, tracking, and sound track in film; the extension of senses through tools like the microscope, telescope, and camera; the measurement of information gathered through senses by statistic analysis and graphing; and the development of an inner eye and ear to probe the subconscious.

A *capstone course,* drawing together insights and skills derived from the entire core curriculum or even the whole 4-year course of study, is by its very nature interdisciplinary. Its position in the curriculum highlights the importance given to it by the university. It is meant to be more important than any other single course. But its time constraints make it less influential than the departmental major cluster of courses or even a set of interdisciplinary courses built into the core curriculum—all of which gradually build mind-sets, develop skills, and reinforce values over more than one semester (LaFauci & Richter, 1970, pp. 51-52).

SCHOOL-WITHIN-A-SCHOOL TEAMS

A school-within-a-school team has teachers from different disciplines instructing a common set of students over an extended period of time, usually 2 to 4 years. This has the advantages of interdisciplinary teams but also builds an esprit de corps among the students. They often eat, play, and pray together as well as study and attend class. Sometimes students and teachers live and have offices in the same halls. Teachers can get to know the students better by observing them in a variety of settings over an extended period of time. Teams of students cutting across disciplines can engage in supervised long-term research projects, growing in both analysis and synthesis skills. Veteran students can become teaching assistants, deepening the quality of their own learning (Singer, 1964).

Apart from providing information, the impact of such a college within a college on students' attitudes and values varies according to several factors:

1. The frequency of contact with another person or group sharing the same interests and goals
2. The number of areas of shared activity (e.g., living, studying, working, playing, eating, social service; participation in setting and enforcing policy)
3. The size of the group sharing the same interests and goals. Small groups encourage all to participate and interact in formal and informal ways, thus exposing members to more challenges to rethink attitudes and values
4. The degree to which the group is isolated, whether physically (dormitories, rural setting) or culturally (self-consciously held values perceived as making the group different from a larger society). This is a ghetto effect, "we-they"
5. The importance assigned by the group and the faculty to the values shared
6. The cooperation within the group (e.g., joint projects; student-to-student teaching or tutoring; involvement in curriculum or course planning and design)
7. The degree of peer-group and faculty interaction with one another frequently, intimately, and in various ways: lounges, libraries; joint committees; colloquia followed by lunch or a visit to the teacher's home; research tutorials where faculty and students learn together
8. The extent to which the project is integrated with other aspects of students' lives (e.g., work, study, community life, personal experience, and interdisciplinary courses) and is real, useful, and able to be done by students
9. The extent to which individual faculty have internalized the goals of the department and/or university
10. The faculty balance. Junior faculty are often more attractive and teach lower-division or undergraduate courses; senior faculty provide identification with pres-

tigious models, are more concerned about basic problems of the field and gathering disciples, and lead the students to question values, lifestyle, and job. They also show how to do so rationally and to think before acting

11. The extent to which teaching, testing, and grading focus on the practice and skills of analysis, synthesis, and critical judgment through experience, discussion, and critical essays, rather than memorizing information. The more active the student, the more learning occurs

12. The overall climate of a university. This has more impact than any other departmental subgroup or even the personality of the student

Breaking out of the taken-for-granted single-subject, single-course, single-teacher pattern encourages other innovations and experiments. For example, students can be split along or across lines of major, gender, age, culture, or other interests, then recombined to stimulate reflection. Remedial programs and honors sections provide other attractive opportunities for use of teams to make available appropriate and effective curricula for students with special needs or interests. They can address different study skills and learning techniques. Again, class assignments can be rotated among different student teams to encourage student interaction, build community, and stimulate learning:

- Environmentalists prepare the room and chalkboard before and after class.
- Greeters welcome others graciously.
- Class mood can be briefly set by poetry or prose, music or song, art or film.
- The content of the previous class is covered in a brief report. It may be oral or on an overhead or poster or wall chart.
- A critique briefly covers the process of the previous class—what happened, what worked or not and why, how well all participated and how they were treated.
- Connections are highlighted between subject areas.
- Applications to life are pointed out. (See Buckley, 1976, for a fuller discussion.)

NOTE

1. Conflict management and resolution are discussed in Chapter 9.

Team Formation and Function

How to Lead the Team

LEADERSHIP TASKS

The role of the leader is to energize, mobilize, and organize the group. What must leaders know and do to be effective?

According to John Gardner in *No Easy Victories* (1968), a good leader should

- Be a symbol of the moral unity of the group.
- Take responsibility to advance the common good of the group.
- Take action against whatever threatens the group effort.
- Identify the problems, challenging members to think creatively.
- Focus attention on the issues, not the personalities of others.
- Help clarify choices.
- Symbolize, voice, and confirm group values.
- Kindle hope.
- Care about the continuing vitality of the group, maintaining and fostering community, mutual appreciation, and a sense of gratitude, pride, and joy.

Steven Covey (1991) has mapped out how leaders promote development of the group through certain stages:

1. Move members from dependence to independence, from infancy to adolescence.
   - Be proactive, not reactive. Take the initiative; don't just wait for things to happen.
   - Clarify goals. Fuzzy goals guarantee confused efforts.
   - Put first things first. Prioritize. Decide where to focus energies.
2. Move members from independence to interdependence, from adolescence to maturity.
   - Think win-win. Think abundance, not scarcity. Instead of compromise, where each loses something, find an approach where each advances genuine values.

True values reinforce one another and multiply their effects. They do not compete.

- Seek to understand rather than to be understood. Repeat to the other's satisfaction. Focus on listening before speaking.
- Synergize—bring everyone to the table. Diversity enriches.
- Sharpen the saw—keep growing intellectually, emotionally, and spiritually.

3. Shift structures from autocracy to
   - Subsidiarity, moving decisions to the lowest possible level
   - Co-responsibility, sharing power to multiply it
   - Consultation, to get as much useful input as possible before deciding
   - Codetermination, so that all affected by a decision share in making it
   - Collaboration, so that all play their parts in carrying out decisions

Loughlan Sofield in *The Collaborative Leader* (1995) described what is needed:

1. Have a process to surface group needs and gifts—and bring them together.
2. Have the skills needed, those listed by Gardner (1968) and Covey (1991).
3. Articulate a vision of identity and mission of past roots and future possibilities, of where the group is coming from and where it is going.
4. Have maturity and generativity, moving beyond the search for personal identity.
5. Work where the team can make a difference. Start small and expand.
6. Humor relativizes seriousness and responsibility and increases trust and productivity. Teams that relax together accomplish more.
7. Confront the main obstacles to teamwork:
   - *Low self-esteem,* which breeds insecurity, competition, and hostility
   - *Burnout,* a form of depression that comes from unrealistic expectations of others and self, as if the team could do whatever it wanted
   - *Failure to deal with loss or failure* by grief, saying goodbye
   - *Fear of conflict.* This is inevitable, but it can be creative and can stimulate imagination. Creative tension is fruitful: Electricity needs both positive and negative poles. Conflict resolutions skills are needed.
   - *Dealing with anger poorly,* letting it become hostility. Instead, forgive.
   - *Lack of shared vision*
   - *Self-righteousness.* Imputing motives to others excuses dropping out.
   - *Poor communication within the team*

Communication builds community. Communication in a teaching team depends on five factors: the speaker, message, medium, listener, and response.

Someone opens the conversation with something to say but in conveying anything reveals something about him- or herself. The message may be information or self-expression, intended to inform, persuade, or entertain. To be effective, it must be put in a language (words, gestures, pictures) that the hearer can understand. The listener is limited by ability to give attention at the time, by emotional blocks or prejudices, and by ability to understand the medium of expression. The communication process is completed by a response or feedback: "Yes" or "No" or "Tell me more." This keeps the conversation going.

Therefore, to communicate effectively, a leader must get to know the team and speak to their hopes, dreams, fears, loves, hates, needs, interests, cultures, and gender differences—to get and hold their attention, build trust, and overcome communication blocks. Wise leaders put their messages in an appealing way, use a language all can understand, and find a time and place where team members are available.

LEADERSHIP STYLES

How do team leaders think of themselves? As decisive and unquestioned military leaders or as judges? As wise and experienced pilots or as stage directors? As harmonizing choir directors or as symphony conductors? As department store managers or as politicians?

Not all leaders operate the same way. Leadership styles will vary on a continuum from autocratic to democratic. Depending on the amount and quality of participation in decision making, power is centralized or diffused.

C						D
E						I
N						F
T						F
R						U
A	1	2	3	4	5	U
L						S
I						E
Z						D
E						
D						

The five points on this spectrum of leadership styles may be described as follows:

1. At one extreme, the leaders identify a problem, consider alternatives, make the decision, and announce it. Subordinates play no role in decision making. They simply follow orders. Power "trickles down."
2. After making a decision, the leader may explain it. Such leaders want more than compliance. If subordinates understand the reasons and goals and accept the decision, their cooperation will be more intelligent and effective.

3. After, or even before making a tentative decision, leaders may invite reactions and input. But they reserve the final decision to themselves. Such managers value the experience and insights of team members. They are willing to listen and learn.
4. The leader may present a problem and ask the group to analyze the situation and decide. Authority is delegated—but only within the limits of the identified problem.
5. The group may identify and diagnose problems, develop possible solutions, and reach a joint decision. The leader may or may not join the discussion, but if present will simply assist the process—and back the decision.

Notice how these approaches vary from coercive and competitive to consultative and collaborative. Unilateral goal setting, decision making, motivation, and control may shift to interactive communication and mutual influence. All of these approaches have been used in university settings (LaFauci & Richter, 1970; see also Beggs, 1964b, pp. 16-22).

How much authority is delegated will depend on various factors: the leader's value system, feelings of security, and confidence in the team and the team's interest in the problem, experience with similar problems, and desire to assume responsibility. Other factors are the complexity of the problem, the time available, and the degree of participation favored by the particular college culture. Not all decisions merit involving the whole group.

SOURCES OF LEADERSHIP

There are three possible sources of leadership:

1. *Status.* The leader is appointed because of connections, regardless of the needs of those served. Order, control, and stability are valued more than group growth. Power and decision making are vertical, centralized in the leader. Trust and confidence in others are minimal. Coercion may be threatened or used. Decisions "trickle down." Teaching emphasis is on uniformity of predetermined content and fulfillment of course requirements. Progress is charted by periodic common examinations. There is little opportunity for innovation.
2. *Functional competence, talent.* The highest value is achievement, getting results—in a broad sense. Competition is used to detect talents and promote progress, measured in terms of research, publications, and teaching effectiveness of faculty. Student progress is measured by test scores and career performance after graduation. Power is readily delegated to those with talents to get things done. Change is encouraged. Students and faculty evaluate each other.
3. *Community orientation.* Leaders are appointed or elected because of charismatic skills in getting people to interact personally and share values. They influence others by eloquence or example. The highest values are not stability or achievement but group growth. There is a high level of trust, confidence, and communication between all members. Power is horizontal, delegated and diffused throughout the group. All members assume listening, challenging, and healing roles as needed. De-

cisions "bubble up" and are reached through consensus whenever possible. Risk taking is encouraged because people learn through mistakes. Intellectual and emotional progress is measured by artistic as well as oral and written expression.

Often all three styles are combined. The same person can use different approaches on different occasions. But when membership in a group is voluntary, community-building skills are essential.

COMMUNITY BUILDING

To form a community, the leader proclaims a vision or ideal or value to people who are psychologically ready, in language that they easily understand. The leader highlights the connections of the vision to values that the others already cherish. The people are attracted, understand the vision, accept it, and commit themselves to it.

The commitment of the group is reinforced by activities. The leader mediates, recognizes the gifts of group members, listens to what is said and not said, senses the mood of the group, and gets members to listen and speak, cooperate and compete, and relate cohesively to other groups.

Delegation of authority does not divide responsibility. It multiplies it. This enables decisions to be made at the level of those most familiar with the problem and most affected by proposed solutions. To foster community, all those affected by a decision should have some say in deciding.

Leaders interested in building community encourage the group to develop and evaluate structures to promote members' personal gifts and to meet the needs of the group. Leaders tend to discourage activities that question the ideal, weaken the commitment, or drain energies from the group.

CHOOSING A LEADERSHIP STYLE

Team teaching normally aims at forming a cohesive group with a high level of motivation, individual initiative, mutual trust, and cooperation. The teachers will model what they want the students to become. The goal of the education project is change, improving the learning process. Teaching fosters learning, the growth of both teachers and students. Short-term goals of increased information and skills are integrated with long-term goals of the interests and perspectives characteristic of the disciplines, character formation, open-mindedness, and sound judgment.

What leadership style will the team find most acceptable? Hidden assumptions about the human dynamics of the team and about what is expected of team members, leaders, teachers, and students can undercut the project and frustrate everyone. It is far better to bring up doubts, fears, enthusiasms, and desires ahead of time. Why are the members on the team? Will all team members be free to question, react, agree, and disagree frankly? How often will the team assess results?

In choosing a leadership style, it is useful to consult the team members about their preferences first. It will also help if they consider the longer range results—on the students, on the administration, and on teachers in similar courses. What advice would they offer to future colleagues? What advice could they get from seasoned veterans? From neutral observers? From those opposed to team teaching? What works best? Why? Will this differ in intradisciplinary courses and interdisciplinary courses? In different cultures? Will the teaching team be more like a family or a sports team? Should leadership be rotated?

LEADERSHIP QUALITIES

The following are desirable leadership qualities. Before the semester, the leader should

- Arrange team membership well in advance
- Organize planning sessions
- Proclaim an attractive vision
- Be personally committed to the project
- Encourage creativity
- Help the team decide the level and frequency of student involvement

During the team meetings, the leader should

- Lead discussion with openness, sensitivity, and humor
- Provide useful suggestions and resources
- Crystallize ideas and decisions
- Initiate action
- Organize project tasks and agenda
- Delegate responsibility widely
- Give clear directions

After the team meetings, the leader should

- Systematically and promptly follow up on decisions
- Maintain records
- Manage details
- Network with the administration and others to get support

9

How to Handle
Conflict on the Team

We have all experienced disharmony within ourselves, with another, with a group, or between groups. Teaching teams must become familiar with the dynamics of conflict so that they can address it effectively within the team itself and with the student groups being taught. Figure 9.1 shows some possible outcomes of conflict.

Although a permanent *negative* view of persons and community creates a negatively charged atmosphere of cynicism resistant to growth, a placid, *uncritical* view of persons and community that is never upset or challenged also leads to stagnation and sterility. Conflict can bring about new dimensions: new insights leading to enrichment and growth. This is true in politics, business, and education. It is one of the major reasons that team teaching is so effective (Gmelch, 1993).

If *properly* handled, conflict within the team or among students can stimulate better communion, through clarity and communication, empathy, maturity, integration or harmony of values, and pluralism, leading to creativity and growth. But if *improperly* handled, conflict can destroy community through closing of minds and hearts, hostility and aggression, self-centeredness, exclusion or expulsion, or stagnation.

According to Freud, conflict can arise from pressure within the personality: the impulses within the *id,* the restraints imposed by parents and society (*super-ego*), and the attempts of reason (*ego*) to assert initiative and control. Figure 9.2 shows sources of conflict according to these three dimensions of self.

One's "point of view" is shaped by various forces that help one establish a personal hierarchy of values and influence one's decisions.

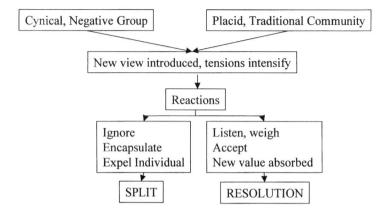

Figure 9.1. Outcomes of Conflict

Superego	Outside pressures: education, laws, customs	Image of what is proper
Ego	Experience/judgment	Image of myself
Id	Inside pressures: moods, basic needs, instincts	Subject vision: "my" point of view

Figure 9.2. Sources of Conflict

When one looks at a value in the context of making a decision, the value will be colored in different ways, creating conflict within the personality. For example, in choosing a career, I may consider my talents, interests, financial prospects, and family traditions and support. A career in ballet may be personally attractive, but how well can I compete? If I do not try it, will I always feel frustrated? How can I clarify and prioritize my values? How can I integrate them?

Pressures from outside—time, friends, work—also can create stress. Education and culture may conflict with what experience has taught, creating a feeling of false guilt. For example, I know by experience that I need 8 hours of sleep each night, but I have been trained to work 14 hours a day; if I don't, I feel lazy and ashamed.

Basic personal needs (security—rest, food—affection, acceptance, integration, growth) or moods (depressed, elated, angry, afraid, jealous, hopeful) may incline a person one way, but the ego (one's self-image and judgment of what is ultimately good for self and others) may urge one to a superior value: to give help, to practice discipline.

Conflict is often between real values, not only between good and evil. Discernment is needed to distinguish values from nonvalues and to establish the relative importance of values. (Conflict over petty values may be a waste of time and energy.)

Failure to resolve important conflicts can result in anger, depression, neuroses, and psychosomatic illness.

Each person caught in the conflict seeks to strengthen his or her own position by reading, consulting, and finding friends to uphold his or her position. The "expression" of the value may become more important than the value itself ("It's the principle of the thing"). The desire to win can lead one to lose sight of the basic issue.

Each sees only one portion of the vision of others. In a group, the members of one faction talk a great deal among themselves *about* the others but do not talk at all *to* the opposing faction. The more they talk to those who agree, the less they want to talk to the opponents. Each side says, "They have closed minds. . . . They do not want to be challenged. . . . They see no value in dialogue."

The results are predictable:

- *Explosion*: Rupture, revolution, enmity.
- *Suppression*:
    1. Separation or expulsion; each goes his or her own way.
    2. One side wins; the other gives up. Some value is lost.
    3. There is coexistence and tolerance, without community.
- *Possible Resolution*:
    1. Compromise. Each gives up something—not ideal.
    2. Discovery of the real values and rights of others.
    3. Integration of both values; healing of memories.
    4. Creativity, building new structures together.

How can the team with the leader find the best solution to the conflict?

- *Exodus.* Get into the other's shoes, inside the other's skin; try to see and feel as the other does. Role-play; switch sides in the debate.
- *Revelation.* Get to the real issues, the values underlying the conflict. Ask, "What are your needs? What pressures are you under right now? What do you treasure? What are you afraid of? What do *you* think the issue is?" *Listen* to the end. *Repeat* what you heard to be sure you understood both the ideas and the feelings. Invite the others to *clarify* what they meant.

- *Empathy.* In words or signs, communicate "feeling with" the other. Try to build lines of communication: a third person, a written explanation, a shared experience outside the area of conflict (e.g., a picnic), a shared responsibility, even a common enemy.
- *Goal Setting.* All must be headed in the same direction before a fruitful discussion of how to get there is possible.
- *Covenant.* If the other person is now ready to make the exodus, present your point of view, needs, pressures, fears, and values.
- If there is no listening or empathy on the other side, wait, but do not give up.

The mediator/leader facilitates the exodus, revelation, empathy, goal setting, and covenant. He or she

- Sees both the positive and negative, the values and limits of each side.
- Can communicate effectively: clearly, without threatening.
- Creates an atmosphere of mutual receptivity through
  - Sense of timing—does not rush or force but builds trust.
  - Sense of humor—games and jokes that appeal to the child on both sides.
- Listens and talks patiently, highlighting the positive points of each side.
- Points out areas of overlapping interests so that values can be integrated.
- Appeals to creativity, discovery, and the challenge of greatness.
- Establishes dialogue so that both sides now talk directly.
- Gets people to play and work together, deepening trust.
- Encourages all to agree on a process and policies for handling disputes.

Developing these skills does more than ease friction. It builds enthusiasm for working together (Weimer, 1993).

How to Train the Team

Initial planning for team teaching was treated in Chapter 3. But once the project is under way, training should intensify. The very process of prioritizing goals and strategies, of experimenting, evaluating, and redesigning the program, leads teachers working on a team to recognize the complexity of the task in which they are engaged.

EDUCATIONAL BACKGROUND

Teachers below the college level are usually required by state law to have some background in the theory and practice of education. They have had at least minimal exposure to courses on how to teach.

Ironically, university professors are at a great disadvantage. They often step into the classroom armed only with their knowledge of their field and their experience of how their teachers in elementary, secondary, and higher education taught them. If they were lucky, they had some excellent role models. If not, they learned what not to do. But they never deliberately thought through the purpose and forms of education, how students learn, and how to help them learn more effectively. Experience forces faculty to deal with these issues, at least sporadically. Over the years, they gradually learn what works.

New teachers are tempted to repeat what they had observed as college or graduate students. They may borrow and mimic or adapt their colleagues' syllabi. In some departments, they will find mentors. But their training for their profession as teachers remains haphazard. Most universities leave them to their own devices.

IN-SERVICE EDUCATION

Teaching teams provide a wonderful opportunity to fill in the gaps in the teachers' education. Senior professors discuss with their junior colleagues the core issues in education, the what and the how. They do this not in a purely theoretical way but in the context of deciding how to teach specified subject matter to a given set of students so that they will learn certain essential content, master certain skills, and develop certain attitudes and values. The whole approach is thoroughly pragmatic, which is how adults learn best.

Membership on a teaching team provides strong motivation to learn more about cognitive psychology and how to use and evaluate different teaching methods. Without having to take special courses in these fields, faculty who discuss teaching goals and means within a team will want to make meaningful contributions to the discussion. This means they will have to do some homework and become familiar with developmental psychology, communications arts, teaching techniques, and educational technology. This research is a form of self-training. More formal training presents opportunities to learn or recall various *"tricks of the trade"*: use of eye contact, moving around the room, using a microphone effectively, audiovisual possibilities, shortcuts for handling attendance records, printing rather than dictating essential data.

Good syllabi do not happen by chance. The team can design and revise syllabi in the light of what they want the course to accomplish. As they discuss the sequence of content, the selection of required and recommended reading, the timing and style of tests, the use of audiovisual material to complement the lectures, and the frequency and focus of small-group discussions, the team members are in effect training one another to be better teachers.

Selection of learning activities draws out of the team members both unexamined assumptions and the fruit of experience. The benefits of special quizzes, case studies, field trips, guided research, discussion groups, contests, and student presentations in debate or dramatic or video form can be explored in training sessions, with perhaps some practice classes critiqued by the team.

Team teaching presents a special problem in grading essays. What strikes one teacher as creative imagination may seem off the point to another. Experience has shown that teachers may differ by more than one letter grade in assessing student work. What to do?

Averaging the difference between the grades is at best a stopgap measure. A third reader could be assigned, and the difference between the two closest grades could be given. Better, the teachers could discuss their reasons for their grades and reach agreement. Even more useful would be some training in grading essays more objectively and systematically. Such training could be built into the general preparation for team teaching. It should at least be given before essays begin to be graded.

WORKSHOPS AND OTHER TRAINING HELPS

The team may feel the need to supplement their own individual research with specialized *workshops* to help the entire team. Some workshops might concentrate on the disciplines being taught. Others could address elements of the process of learning and teaching, of grading and discipline. Still others could provide psychological and sociological analyses of the students, bringing into awareness issues that the faculty might have thought of only in passing. All of this is a more formal sort of training, valuable both to team members and to other faculty.

The most profitable workshops are those given for extended periods during the summer. These may be beyond the budget of the school. But occasional workshops can be scheduled during the year. The best workshops schedule time not only for input from outside experts but also for local teachers to talk about their own experiences and feelings and to try out new techniques. Taping or videotaping practice sessions provides opportunities for everyone to make comments and suggestions on how to do even better.

Training videos and CD-ROMs are available for many topics connected with team teaching: communication, conflict resolution, change management, creativity, continuous self-improvement, motivation, multimedia use, and time and stress management. Workshops could be built around these professionally prepared materials for the entire faculty.

Other training might be aimed directly at the teaching teams. Content for these training sessions will surface as the team evaluates its own work. Communications facilitators might be invited to sit in on team sessions and suggest more productive use of the time allotted to meetings. Education specialists could train the team to capitalize on its strengths and remedy its weaknesses.

The frequency and length of team planning sessions directly affect learning outcomes for teachers and students. Any kind of in-depth discussion takes time and cannot be finished in a single meeting. Finding time when the entire team will be free is always problematic as soon as the team expands beyond two or three teachers. This becomes even more difficult if outside specialists must be scheduled, but the results are worth the effort. New plateaus of insight and cooperation are reached. Otherwise, team interaction remains superficial, and the full potential of working together remains unexploited.

What topics are addressed in planning sessions? Learning outcomes, syllabi, texts, teaching styles, assessment, grading, motivation, discipline, administrative support, team membership and participation. The list will be extended according to the interests of the team.

Participation in the team itself becomes a form of training in group dynamics: brainstorming, listening with respect, suggesting rather than imposing, praising and supporting others' ideas, reaching consensus or at least agreeing to try an experiment enthusiastically. Many virtues are learned, especially humility, patience, and graciousness. Some teams deliberately include a counselor, at least occasionally, not only to alert the teachers to student issues but also to help them improve interaction within the team. As teachers experience community-building skills, they more readily employ them in class.

The purpose of a teaching team, like that of a production or marketing team, is to complete a task. The chief goal is not to form community. However, the building of close personal relationships and a team spirit, the learning of skills in interaction, and the formation of a feeling of mutual trust can all contribute to the better accomplishment of the task. Some groups prefer more intimacy, others less. This will depend on the free choices of the members. Team members do not have to be close friends. Each team must develop its own working climate. For some, training in the principles of building community may help.

Team members learn by observing one another in action in the classroom. This on-the-job training can be intensified if teammates get together after such sessions and pool notes on what worked best and why. Some teams have made videotapes of lectures and discussion groups so that the teachers can see and hear themselves as others do. The videos can be reviewed privately or in team sessions—but only after sufficient camaraderie has been established.

Team teaching can train teachers in a continuing internship program. Interns can assume minimum teaching responsibilities during their first year. This gives them time to attend other classes, participate in team and department activities, and develop close personal contact with other team members. Bit by bit, they engage in the give-and-take of the team self-reflection. They learn their own strengths and weaknesses and those of other team members, and how to address those issues constructively (LaFauci & Richter, 1970).

Training can help teachers on a team to be more effective in inspiring, directing, and monitoring students engaged in individual research. One of the benefits of teamwork is that large-group sessions can free teachers and students to do more than just work through a fixed syllabus. Different teachers will establish rapport with different students, but the whole team can suggest research and publication possibilities that would never have occurred to the students by themselves. Bit by bit, the students develop more independence and responsibility.

TIME MANAGEMENT

Training can help teachers establish better habits of time management. This is valuable for all teachers but is especially helpful for members of a teaching team because work on the team can devour large blocks of time. These techniques can be used inside the classroom, too, to break up long periods into bite-sized pieces. Wise instructors recognize the need for a change of pace to keep the students' attention. Once the teachers master the skills for managing time, they can pass them on to the students.

Team members can be trained to have a few "5-minute lectures" in their portfolio to fill in periods when they have successfully taught what they planned faster than they had anticipated. Or they may use a spot quiz to find out what the students found most clear, most valuable, or still confusing. Extra time provides an opportunity to address some issue that surfaced in several student papers or even to ask students for suggestions on how to improve the course.

LECTURES AND DISCUSSIONS

Training can raise the level of all teaching methods. Teams can be trained to give more high-quality lectures, mixing audiovisuals (overlays, audio- and videotapes, CD-ROMs, Web pages) with verbal pointers on what to look for and listen to and how to take notes. They can personalize this by adding their own organization of key ideas along with local and topical applications.

Training provides techniques to improve the focus and participation of discussion groups. Most students profit by organizing their thoughts and putting their ideas into words. Discussion leaders can be trained to encourage all students to take part in the conversation, to listen so closely that they can paraphrase others' statements, to try to find the truth in what others say, and to affirm as well as criticize.

Listening to the discussion, the teacher spots what students have learned from the lecture, how they react to it, and how the lecture can be improved next time. Teachers find out what stimulates students and what stupefies. They also discover a wealth of information that can improve their customization of the course to a specific group of students.

The training program can include general faculty meetings in which team members give presentations about their own experiences and what they have learned about the strengths and weaknesses of this method. The faculty could be broken into small discussion groups to explore problems more thoroughly and to get feedback from all the teachers. Records should be kept to underscore the seriousness with which comments are treated. Many new insights will arise, enthusiasm will grow, and others will volunteer for team teaching. Bulletins or newsletters can share these findings with a wider audience (Beggs, 1964a, pp. 37-40, 45-47).

Another form of training is for teachers to visit other classes, whether taught by team members or not. They can observe, noting new techniques and then trying them out either individually or with the team. In this way, learning is not confined to one school but can spread to others. It helps to have a checklist of what to look for and how to critique it.

Conferences off campus also provide opportunities for observing other professionals so that teachers get some feel for what to expect. They can report their findings to team or department members.

MORALE

Morale is an important factor in experimenting with any new approach to teaching. As Western Electric discovered at its Hawthorne plant, virtually any change in working conditions produced initial enthusiasm: The workers saw change in their routine as a sign that management cared about them. This did not prove the intrinsic superiority of the new arrangement. Evidence of that appeared only after the decline of the initial enthusiasm. For the boost in energy to continue, management had to provide ongoing signs of interest and support.

This is true of team teaching also. Enthusiasm in beginning this new approach gets the team over the first hurdles of accepting peer criticism. But team members must find ways of frequently complimenting one another and recognizing the beneficial results for both teachers and students. Administrators, too, can remark periodically on the progress made and on their plans for team teaching in the future. This builds a sense of achievement and healthy self-satisfaction.

Rotation of team members, whether by normal attrition or by deliberate choice of the faculty or administration, contains built-in elements of training. Former team members enrich other teams or their departments with their experiences. New team members must be brought up to speed. They will need some orientation to the entire process and its salient factors.

The transition from intradisciplinary to interdisciplinary teamwork merits special attention. It is relatively easy for a couple of professors teaching the same course to agree on limited and informal cooperation. Working with several teachers of different disciplines takes much more complex coordination. The shift is facilitated and simplified by adequate planning beforehand and by some ongoing training on the integration of content matter and methods.

Teams may occasionally get together with other teams from the same or different departments to discuss what they have learned or even plan joint projects. This makes the move from intradisciplinary to interdisciplinary teams much easier.

One of the most important sources of training is the process of decision making within the team. This will be discussed in the next chapter (Chamberlin, 1969, pp. 55-59).

Evaluation is a necessary element in achieving constant improvement. This in itself provides training through reflection, critique, and planned change. The entire process of assessment will be addressed at length in Chapter 12.

11

How to Make
Decisions as a Team

All kinds of issues relating to team teaching require decision making: the selection of the members; preparing syllabi; learning outcomes, teaching styles, assessment, and grading; and the frequency, content, and management of meetings before and during the course of the semester. Beyond the minimal level of two teachers combining their class sessions, the success of team teaching depends on joint planning sessions. The team will be composed of people with different personalities and teaching styles, perhaps different philosophies of education and expectations of students, probably with a mix of age, gender, and culture. If the team is to operate smoothly, members must agree on some basic principles of communication and cooperation in making decisions (Chamberlin, 1969, pp. 55-59).

STYLES OF DECISION MAKING

Decisions can be reached in three ways: imposition, compromise, or integration. *Imposition* (win-lose) tends to build resentment among the losers because one side wins and the other loses. *Compromise* may result in the loss of important insights or values. Both sides win something and lose something. *Integration* is the ideal, in which all sides win, but it may not always be feasible.

The stimulus for a decision may come from a superior, from a subordinate, from a peer, or from within the person deciding. The inner stimulus is the most creative. It is also the most valuable in a teaching team, most likely to lead to genuine integration (Barnard, 1938, pp. 189-192).

SYSTEMS APPROACH

Team planning continuously centers on people, money, position, time, and physical facilities. A systems approach lowers the likelihood that anyone will jump to conclusions under the pressure of the moment. A system is a procedure that can be understood and followed by all concerned. If the team has thought through all the dimensions of a problem and everyone has been consulted, the final decision is more likely to be accepted and implemented.

The following is a workable problem-solving system for a teaching team:

1. Identify the problem and its causes.
2. Gather pertinent information.
3. Brainstorm possible solutions.
4. Weigh the solutions, foreseeing probable consequences.
5. Choose the solution most likely to lead to integration of all of the values desired.
6. Develop an action plan.
7. Implement the plan.
8. Evaluate the results and redesign the plan.

This is much like the system that was proposed in Chapter 3 to design the original program for team teaching. Some such system is particularly valuable when a team faces any serious, complex problem. There is no point in wasting time and energy on decisions unless they are relevant and workable, unless the time is right to make them, and unless the team has the authority to make them.

OBJECTIVITY

Because the team members will be personally involved in the analysis and outcomes, many subjective factors may cloud the decision-making process. In the interests of a more objective diagnosis, the group should try stepping back to see the larger picture and all the issues involved. This will help them to gauge the real importance of the problem so that it is not blown out of proportion. It will also jog their imagination to consider factors they may have overlooked—or to avoid considerations that are really trivial or not ripe for action.

Some other techniques for achieving objectivity are imagining the advice that an outside consultant, whether a generalist or a specialist, would give; imagining the advice that the team members would give to others facing a similar problem; or imagining how an accreditation team would evaluate their decision. It helps also to imagine how opponents might attack the plan, overall or in details. A team member might be appointed "devil's advocate" to present as strong as possible a case for the other side.

Who else, familiar with the situation, could give an impartial view? How would it look to an administrator, a parent, an alumnus, a politician? To someone in a different historical or professional or cultural setting?

SUBJECTIVITY

Instead of setting emotions aside, try intensifying them. Imagine how the students will feel about this. How will the proposal fit into their values and mindsets? To be successful, the team members should anticipate their reactions and tap into the power of their emotions. The team should show students how the solution will benefit them, improve learning and morale, eliminate the unimportant to focus on essentials, and save time and effort in the long run.

It is useful to recall how this problem resembles past challenges and what previous approaches were successful. To avoid repeating past mistakes from here or elsewhere, the team might compare their problem to an analogous situation in another school or culture or even profession.

The problem might be broken down into subproblems that can be tackled more successfully one by one, starting with the easiest. Members could ponder how to simplify and eliminate factors or substitute and replace elements. This approach can reveal significant patterns involving time, place, materials, technologies, people, skills, activities, or failures.

A solution might be more likely if the staff were increased or better trained or motivated. Could role models or peers help? The team might brainstorm with opponents, then negotiate to reach a mutually acceptable position.

Another approach might be to divide the work and assign tasks according to the skills, interests, and styles of the people involved. Prioritize the resources of time, information, money, equipment, and supplies they need. Figure out how to get them. Map out an action plan of steps in sequence.

In short, it is important to bring to the surface as many as possible of the various factors that affect the decision-making process:

- The goals and values, conscious or subconscious, of team members
- The interests of various other groups in the outcome (students, administrators, parents, government)
- Limits set by money, time, buildings, and regulations

The team does not make its decisions in a vacuum. A school, like the human body, is made up of numerous interlocking systems or networks, all interdependent. Just as in the body the circulatory system, respiratory system, digestive system, reproductive system, central nervous system, autonomic nervous system, immune system, and temperature-regulating system all interact to preserve overall health, so too faculty, students, administrators, support staff, alumni, parents, and even outside regulatory agencies cooperate to produce the highest-quality education available in a certain time and place for a given amount of resources. All these groups have legitimate interests in the outcomes, especially when what is done in the classroom will have repercussions throughout the entire network of the school, or even beyond. They would like to be involved in the decisions that will affect the education being offered.

Just as all those who would be affected by a decision should be involved in making that decision, so too they should all be informed of the decision once it is made. Whenever possible, they should be given the rationale behind the decision. They should also be told that the results will be evaluated and the plan revised if necessary. This feedback manifests respect for all the persons involved. It maintains the good will of all concerned and lessens the likelihood of resistance.

Evaluation and Support

12

How to Evaluate the Team

The evaluation of team teaching is part of an overall strategy of universitywide self-scrutiny. Accreditation agencies demand that the entire university engage in an ongoing assessment in all areas: teaching, learning, fund-raising, student services, and administration. The board of trustees is to evaluate the president, the president is to evaluate the work of all the vice presidents, and so on down the chain of command. The accrediting bodies want to ensure the health of the universities, the academic standards of the professional communities, and the ultimate benefit of the nation and the world.

In contemporary culture, all universities are competing for students and foundation grants. They must produce some evidence that they are delivering quality education in a cost-effective manner. To produce such proof, not only must they have a clear statement of mission and goals—long range, middle range, short range, and immediate—but they must formulate some plan of how to reach those goals within a reasonable time frame. To know how well the plan is working, they must engage in some form of self-study.

In a university, assessment is a structured process to measure the impact of university programs on students, faculty, and society at large. This involves systematic collection and dissemination of information to enable the evaluators to make reasonable and informed value judgments. What are the strengths and weaknesses of the programs? How can they be improved? What are the criteria for success? How can they be measured? How will the findings be interpreted? How will they be used to foster change? Trustees, administrators, faculty, students, parents, alumni, and representatives of academia in society all have legitimate interests in getting answers to these questions.

Assessment, therefore, is not just one more activity competing with others for attention and resources. It is an all-pervasive project enabling the university to fulfill its mission and to attain its goals in the best possible ways.

Evaluation can be carried on by various methods, such as task forces or permanent committees, surveys of various types, and workshops for all segments of the institution to explain the purpose and methods of self-evaluation. Students, faculty, and administration must all be involved because the process will lead to decisions that will affect the life of the whole university.

Evaluation of team teaching will center on two areas: the impact of this teaching method on the students and on the faculty. These are interrelated but distinct outcomes.

EVALUATING THE IMPACT OF
TEAM TEACHING ON THE STUDENTS

There are hundreds of articles on team teaching but not much scientific research to measure its effects on students. It is difficult to control the significant variables because students do not have to sign up for team-taught courses. Many who do will be biased in favor of the experiment—they will want it to succeed. And so many factors are involved: teacher personalities and teaching styles, use of texts, interaction with other students, available facilities and equipment, and changes of method during the course.

Nevertheless, it is important to try to evaluate achievements and failures, intended and unintended, using reliable and valid instruments to test the students for cognitive, affective, and behavioral outcomes like these:

- Achieve knowledge and understanding of the basic elements, themes, and trends of the course content
- Advance perspectives and knowledge, within or across disciplines, to provide intellectual stimulation
- Address major problems in the field, evaluate past and present solutions, and spur creative future solutions
- Interest, challenge, and motivate students to acquire the desired knowledge, skills, and values of the subject matter of the course and discipline
- Advance personal values and sensitivities, within or across disciplines
- Build appreciation and respect for the dignity and feelings of others
- Instill cultural values and attitudes
- Provide a sense of accomplishment and satisfaction
- Stimulate more personal integration
- Build a sense of community through cooperation
- Provide skills to observe, research, analyze, synthesize, listen, critique, and communicate, including

- Ability to take notes on lectures and readings
- Ability to engage in group discussion with responsibility
- Ability to write and speak clearly and effectively on course content
- Ability to use the essential resources and tools of the discipline to solve typical and new problems
- Ability to do research with critical analysis and judgment
- Ability to use creative imagination in integrating life experience with course content
- Ability to engage fruitfully in interdisciplinary dialogue
- Ability to manage time well and study effectively

The methods also should be evaluated:

- Faculty collaborative planning to achieve the goals
- Clear, interesting, challenging, and appropriate readings
- Clear, interesting, challenging, and appropriate lectures
- Interesting, open, and focused class discussions
- Interesting, challenging, and appropriate research projects, field trips, reports, and papers
- Appropriate and fair examinations
- Cross-listing of the course to satisfy registration, scheduling, grading, and unit value requirements of different departments and colleges
- Contact with fellow students and faculty outside class
- Equipment, physical facilities and environment, including library and Internet
- Frequent feedback to faculty from peers and students about the effectiveness of the various means of reaching the course goals
- Evaluation of the design and effectiveness of the course as a whole

No existing instruments measure all these items. In fact, test designers try to limit the factors measured to as few as possible, lest student interest flag and reliability falter. Yet every one of these factors of the learning experience deserves attention. What to do?

Some programs design a profile of a graduate. Though expressed in narrative form, the desired qualities should be able to be specified along the lines outlined above. A vague picture of an ideal graduate is not very helpful when it comes time to decide what methods should be employed to achieve the desired result. A blurry target guarantees an uncertain aim.

It is not always easy to measure results of a program. Hyman (1970) has summarized the complications:

- Measuring learning outcomes is always inexact. Knowledge of facts can easily be tested. Attitudes, values, and skills are more difficult. Low ratings may be due to many factors outside the teachers' control.

- What can be measured accurately may not be the most important outcome.
- The time that the outcomes should be measured must be determined—for example, immediately after a lesson, a month later, two years after graduation.
- The rating of criteria is quite subjective. Not everyone will agree with descriptions of good, excellent, or outstanding learning. Who determines the criteria? (pp. 276-280)

To begin with, mission statements, which state broad intentions, must be translated into goals and objectives that specify, for example, the desired learning outcomes in terms of knowledge, attitudes, values, skills, and behaviors that can be accurately observed. The measures may include teacher observation of the students in class, objective tests, essays, student papers accepted for publication or for presentation at academic conferences, self-assessments in portfolios, ratings by outside supervisors or employers, acceptance into graduate programs, alumni surveys, or salaries or promotions after graduation.

Although these measures can be quantified, they are not really exact. Many factors can throw off the results. The weather, family problems, or the student's health and mood can affect class participation and test scores. Any published author knows that acceptance of articles by journals is a highly subjective process, even if the review is "blind" and the referees do not know the authors. Self-assessment is rarely impartial. Supervisors and employers may experience all sorts of personality conflicts that affect their perception of others' work. Salaries may reflect not competence but connections.

Different academic programs will have quite distinct learning objectives, measured in many different ways. Music will differ from biology, mathematics from political science, philosophy from modern languages. Each course should have clear learning objectives. If they are put into the syllabi, the students can enter into the learning process more deliberately. They will know where they are supposed to go and how to get there.

Often the feelings and skills desired are not measured accurately by objective tests. It is hard to measure the excitement generated by the clash of teacher viewpoints, the changes of voice and rhythm, the different styles and personalities, the modeling of critical thinking and courteous disagreement, and the exposure to interdependence and correlations between subject areas and between the classroom and life. It is also difficult to calculate students' development of poise in presenting ideas to groups of different sizes or their development of listening skills and discussion skills. But these are very desirable outcomes that lead to lifelong learning.

The students have a right to know what they need to do to earn a particular grade. The teaching team should thoroughly discuss how grades will be given to the students, by whom, and the norms to be used. Acceptable norms might be as follows:

- Undergraduate

  A = Outstanding (beyond a thorough grasp of text and lectures, shows ability to re-late material to life and to other subject areas and to form a personal synthesis; fine critical judgment; good bibliography; very good oral and written expression; excellent candidate to do graduate work in the field)

  B = Superior (thorough grasp of text and lectures; shows critical judgment, good speaking and writing skills; can do graduate work)

  C = Satisfactory (general grasp of texts and lectures; some errors in nonessentials)

  D = Unsatisfactory

  F = Failure (course not counted toward degree requirements)

- Graduate

  A = Outstanding (beyond a thorough grasp of text and lectures, shows great ability to relate material to life and to other subject areas and to form a personal synthesis; shows excellent critical judgment; fine bibliography; highly polished skills in speaking and writing; papers could be published; excellent candidate for doctoral work)

  B = Satisfactory (beyond a thorough grasp of text and lectures, can relate material to life and to other subject areas and can form personal synthesis; shows very good critical judgment in area and choice of bibliography; very good oral and written expression)

  C = Meets minimum standards for obtaining graduate credit

  F = Failure (does not meet minimum standards for obtaining credit)

Scores of students on Graduate Record Examinations, Law School Aptitude Tests, Nursing State Board Examinations, and Bar Examinations, acceptances into graduate programs, and employment records all give some objective insight into progress made in comparison with what is done elsewhere.

In the final analysis, each team must decide what to measure, when, and how. Students, parents, administrators, and accrediting agencies deserve more than educated hunches and wishful thinking about the effectiveness of team teaching. The more attention is focused on learning outcomes, the more fruitful the teaching will be. Teachers will have to devise ways to get at the results as accurately as possible (Weimer, 1993).

Behaviors can be observed. Students can learn to listen and to follow directions. They show this by meeting deadlines and producing papers in the proper format. There is no need for an objective test to measure these skills. If independent thinking is a desirable outcome, it will be demonstrated by questioning, disagreeing, and making creative suggestions in class. To check the ability to interrelate disciplines, one can note such references in student papers and class interventions. The team members can decide how they will detect hard evidence that the students have learned the desired knowledge, skills, and values.

EVALUATING THE IMPACT OF
TEAM TEACHING ON THE TEAM ITSELF

Team members are not only interested in getting the students to learn more. They want to be stimulated themselves to do better teaching: to be more creative in their lectures, with better organization, clearer topic divisions, greater emphasis on the most important areas, and more imaginative use of audiovisuals, and to be more successful in getting students actively engaged in the learning process through questioning, group interaction, and interesting research projects.

Teachers on a team can be enriched through the approaches and ideas of other team members. Their assumptions may be challenged by people with different ethnic backgrounds or sexual orientations. Lively planning sessions can not only improve their performance in the classroom but lead to new research and publication.

The time saved by combining classes can be used to plan lessons, discuss educational psychology, and keep abreast of new developments in the field. This keeps the syllabus current and prevents boredom.

Repeating the same lecture can lead to mental fatigue. Burnout is far less likely on a team. The lectures are critiqued before and after delivery. They may be interrupted by other teachers. Concepts have to be rethought and their sequence changed. All of this is invigorating.

Flexibility expands. Teachers can try out different methods, class sizes, groupings, and time blocks. Specialists, consultants, and resource people are better used. Contemporary sources and applications ensure relevance.

On a team, teachers pool their strengths. Their weaknesses are remedied. They complement one another's expertise. Poor teachers can be observed, critiqued, and improved by the suggestions of other team members in a nonthreatening, supportive context. By watching good teachers, they pick up ideas on how to involve even recalcitrant students. They build community as a team and develop trust as they experience others' patience and help.

Mutual reliance within the team cuts pressures. Burdens shared are cut in half; happiness shared is doubled. Sharing in decision making boosts self-confidence. As the team see the quality of teaching and learning improve, their self-esteem and happiness grow. This rise in morale improves retention and recruitment.

All of these factors deserve to be measured one way or another. The quantification may not be exact, but the results can be palpable, accessible to some sort of analysis that can be reported to groups with legitimate concerns. The study can be conducted by team members or other faculty.

As Hyman (1970) stated, "To observe is one thing; to evaluate, another. . . . Evaluating also involves judging or rating. . . . One must evaluate how performance measures up to a well-defined concept of teaching and teaching responsibilities" (p. 273).[1] This task involves several steps:

1. The evaluator must decide what factors to evaluate. This decision is tied in with the purpose of the evaluation (e.g., to compare the effectiveness of team teaching to that of individual instruction).

2. The evaluator must decide on the criteria that constitute desirable or effective teaching. These criteria are not facts but value judgments subject to rethinking and revision.

3. The evaluator must gather data about the factors to be evaluated or weighed, such as the learning outcomes of the students or teacher interaction or satisfaction.

4. The evaluator must compare the data with the criteria.

5. The evaluator makes a value judgment about the teaching or learning being considered. How good or effective is it? How close does reality match up with the ideal outcome? Before a final decision, the evaluator may wish to reconsider the criteria. (Hyman, 1970, pp. 273-275)

ASSESSMENTS BY STUDENTS, TEACHERS, AND ADMINISTRATORS

Students, like teachers, are involved in the teaching-learning process. They have a right to be actively engaged in the evaluation of the program. Students can assess the course for the relevance, logic, clarity, and interest of presentations, for perceived faculty effectiveness, and for how well, in their own judgment, they learned the values and skills desired.

Various instruments for student evaluations of faculty and courses at the end of the semester have been designed and tested for validity and reliability. But there is no need to wait so long for feedback. Every week or month, students can be asked for critiques of what worked or not and for suggestions on how to improve. Some teachers regularly assign "3-minute papers" in which students state the main idea of the class, the most unclear point, and a question they still have or a point they want to have developed at more length (Angelo & Cross, 1993). Some teams encourage question boxes in the department or team office where comments may be left anonymously. Students are quite accurate in spotting sham, hypocrisy, and unfairness, whether they like a teacher or not.

Self-evaluation by the team can also reveal major problems that must be faced. Some teammates may be incompatible or inflexible or irresponsible. Some may be unwilling to risk failure. Others may find it difficult to learn from mistakes. The process of appointing team members may have to be changed. Planning sessions also take time and energy. Without proper structures, much time and energy can be wasted. Leadership styles may have to be adjusted. Roles may need clarification. Training may need fine tuning. The team may have encountered difficulties with facilities, equipment, and administrative support.

Administrators also should evaluate team teaching, looking at syllabi and lesson plans and the use of audiovisuals and even attending team planning sessions. They should take into account the evaluations of students and teachers but should also focus on other factors, such as scheduling, the use of facilities and equipment, the value of team teaching for orienting new teachers and providing in-service training, the bettering of teaching and research, the improvement of morale, and the reduction of student-teacher personality problems. Administrators must also address costs in their evaluation. Time will be needed for rescheduling faculty and rooms, for team planning, and for dealing with the personality problems and stress that team teaching may bring for the team members. Budgets must be adjusted for adequate classroom and media facilities and additional audiovisual materials. Salaries may have to be changed or release time given for the additional responsibilities undertaken by team members. To cut costs, nonprofessional staff may take over some of the nonteaching responsibilities currently carried by faculty.

COMPARATIVE EVALUATION

The goal of evaluation is to do better. Better than what? What is the alternative? One clear option would be to stay with single-teacher, closed-classroom instruction that has characterized much of college teaching in the first part of this century. It still prevails in many courses and programs today. The impact of such methods on both students and teachers can be studied and compared to the results of team teaching (Bair & Woodward, 1964, pp. 188-215).

The comparison cannot be conclusive and definitive because of the many types of team teaching and the personality traits of the teachers who have tried team teaching and like it. Their enthusiasm may be a contributing factor to its success. Nevertheless, some of them teach both on teams and individually. They can base their observations on firsthand experience.

Other teachers have tried team teaching and dislike it. They, too, should be queried. They, too, can base their observations on firsthand experience.

Only after listening to proponents and opponents, carefully distinguishing the forms of team teaching they describe, and comparing their experiences and judgments can one make a solid prudential decision. Proponents will highlight strengths, opponents will stress weaknesses. Both strengths and weaknesses should be studied and weighed if evaluation is to be honest and complete (see Olivero, 1964, for useful directions on how to set up research designs to obtain internal and external validity).

In making the comparisons, Olivero suggested these questions:

- The Teaching Team
  1. Can teachers operate more effectively as individuals or in teams?
  2. Can personality conflicts be avoided?
  3. Can clerical assistance be utilized effectively?
  4. Can teachers plan their time so they will be able to make additional preparations for improved instruction?
  5. Can esprit de corps be developed among members of the team?
  6. Can teachers assume specialized function responsibility?
- Large Student Groups
  1. Can lectures be presented in a dynamic, meaningful manner?
  2. Can large groups be as effective with 200 students as they can with 50 students?
  3. Can facilities be arranged to provide optimal visual and auditory accommodations?
  4. Can needless repetition of material be avoided?
  5. Can students be motivated in large groups?
- Small Student Groups
  1. Can teachers conduct small groups effectively?
  2. Can teachers identify "power and prestige" figures in the small groups?
  3. Can students profit from an opportunity of verbalizing concepts?
  4. Can values be changed in small groups?
  5. Can students interact with each other?
  6. Can teachers in small groups do a more effective job of identifying and solving individual learning problems?
- Student Instruction
  1. Can students score better on achievement tests?
  2. Can students retain and transfer generalizations, principles, and concepts more effectively?
  3. Can creative learning experiences be provided?
  4. Can students be taught individual responsibility for learning?
  5. Can students of all levels of ability profit from such an organizational structure?
- Human Resources
  1. Can nonschool resource people be more effectively utilized?
  2. Can the advantages in terms of human energy and time balance out the costs?
  3. Can the dropout rate be reduced?
- Financial Resources
  1. Can materials be used more economically?
  2. Can the per-student cost of education be reduced? (pp. 106-107)

Of course, this list would have to be adapted to the local situation and made more detailed. But its questions can be clearly defined and tested. If a school moves slowly into team teaching, it can set up control groups and compare results—immediate, short term, and long term—by tracking students and alumni.

NOTE

1. Hyman (1970, pp. 256-283) presented distinctions between observation, measurement, evaluation, and assessment—all useful for team teaching.

13

How to Improve the Team

Assessment in a university is not done purely for its own sake, to satisfy the curiosity of students or teachers and get a clear picture of what is going on and how well they are doing. Beyond the laudable goal of building self-esteem and self-confidence, evaluation aims at learning from mistakes and improving the quality of the educational experience.

Improvement in team teaching does not just happen. True, there is a natural progression from very simple, two-teacher cooperation to cooperation in more complex groups, often hierarchically arranged, and from intradisciplinary to interdisciplinary teams, as the potentials of this approach are discovered. But even these developments result from formal or informal appraisal of results.

Each year, there will be new students with different backgrounds and different needs in a constantly changing world. The teaching team can never afford to rest in their quest for excellence. Units may have to be added, replaced, or put in a different sequence. The team must find new relationships between concepts and new ways to help students, present material, eliminate unnecessary repetition, and provide needed reinforcement.

Testing is an integral element of the assessment process. If all students score 100% on all tests, the tests are poorly designed. They give no feedback on strengths and weaknesses of students or of teaching methods and no help to make the course more interesting, more memorable, and more effective. Genuine evaluation aims at doing better.

As in science, improvement in teaching flows from a regular cycle: experiment, analyze, evaluate, redesign, reevaluate. Team teaching is an educational experiment designed to improve output. The results must be carefully measured, analyzed, and evaluated so that the process may be redesigned to produce better outcomes. Any increase in productivity or effectiveness in education must be measured in terms of learning outcomes and teaching outcomes.

The following are learning outcomes:

1. Cognitive improvement
   * Know and understand more information
   * Know data more accurately
   * Retain information longer
   * See more connections within the field and across fields
   * Show better judgment, in analysis and synthesis, about the field
   * Formulate more creative hypotheses to advance the field
2. Affective improvement (feelings)
   * Have greater interest and motivation to acquire the desired knowledge, skills, and values of the subject matter of the course and discipline
   * Be more committed to personal values and sensitivities, within or across disciplines
   * Have higher appreciation and respect for the dignity and feelings of others
   * Have deeper cultural values and attitudes
   * Have greater sense of accomplishment and satisfaction
   * Show more personal integration
   * Have a more satisfying sense of community
3. Behavioral improvement (better skills to observe, research, analyze, synthesize, listen, critique, and communicate)
   * Take better notes on lectures and readings
   * Engage in group discussion with greater responsibility
   * Write and speak more clearly and effectively
   * Use the essential resources and tools of the area to solve typical and new problems more fruitfully
   * Do research with better critical analysis and judgment
   * Better integrate life experience with course content
   * Engage more fruitfully in interdisciplinary dialogue
   * Manage time and study more effectively

Improved teaching means more than better learning by students. It also means that the teachers conclude that they have more satisfying teaching conditions:

* More fun and creativity in collaborative planning
* Clearer and more interesting readings and lectures
* More interesting, open, and focused class discussions

- More interesting and challenging research projects, field trips, reports, and papers
- Improved examinations
- More contact with fellow students and faculty outside class, with greater team spirit, using e-mail and telephone
- Better equipment, physical facilities and environment, including library and Internet
- Increased scholarship and publications

SYSTEMATIC STEPS TO TAKE

What must be done to bring about these improvements? Will they happen automatically as teachers and students become more familiar with team teaching? Possibly, but progress can be accelerated by systematically addressing certain elements.

The teaching team must ask itself several questions.

First, *would other material—experiments, lectures, videotapes, films, field trips, readings—work significantly better?* For example, a lecture might be replaced by a film. The film would have several advantages. It would be expensively produced in full color, take the students to a place and time they could not readily visit, and use a script carefully designed to reveal the persons' characters and to highlight the most important facts and lessons to learn. It could be used over and over. On the other hand, it would eliminate the feedback a lecturer gets from students by observing their posture and faces, sensing the classroom atmosphere, and adjusting the pace and content of delivery to match the students' collective mood. It would eliminate any possibility of interruption for clarification and any likelihood of switching direction because of student interests or questions. The team could discuss and weigh these factors.

Second, *could the location or timing or sequence or technologies of certain teaching or learning activities be changed?* What would be the results? Better or worse? Why?

Distance learning poses significant opportunities, within certain limits:[1]

- Two-way interactive video can link classes within the same or up to four time zones so that all the students and teachers can see one another directly.
- If classes meet in different locales separated by one or more time zones, the students and teachers must make and use videos and feel comfortable with e-mail and the Internet. Otherwise special workshops must be provided to allay fears and build skills, including learning how to make "bookmarks" and "nicknames."
- Videos should be made for students at all the sites and sent to one another. Preferably, multiple copies of the videos can be made available through the library, enabling students to view them, like homework, before the class discussions on site.
- E-mail keeps the conversation going outside of class throughout the week and enables people who are shy or do not want to dominate class discussions to express

their ideas carefully, even revising them before sending them. This promotes full participation of all students in class discussions. Over the course of a semester, discussions via e-mail grow in breadth of interest and in depth of content.

- Internet discussion groups—chatrooms, newsgroups—are one step beyond e-mail. They allow "threading": They graphically display who is communicating to whom and how frequently. For this, passwords are essential to maintain security and to build trust and openness.
- Current peculiarities of Netscape can be discouraging to neophytes: using Tab instead of Enter to end a line; the need to maximize the screen and use Options to show all messages; setting up a listserve group (or grouping many addresses under one nickname).
- In the future, distance education servers (DESs) will simplify e-mail, chatrooms, and creation of home pages (with a menu of syllabus, bibliography, biographies and pictures of class members, bookmarks, nicknames, class outlines with Power-Point slides, and simplified access to an electronic discussion group). Waivers (and digital photos) are needed to post pictures on the Internet, using html. In the meantime, Windows 98 with Netscape 3.0 and Corel 97 speed setting up home pages and converting to html files. Shareware by Macromedia compresses files for transmission over the Internet; they then can be converted into html.
- It is very helpful to have students set up the home page during the previous semester.

There are many advantages to a virtual community:

- Communication can take place when and where convenient: home, office, or school.
- The ability to rewrite before sending a message gives a more sophisticated version.
- The natural shyness of inarticulate students can be overcome with proper motivation, including grades.
- Nicknames or listserve groups allow communication with many people simultaneously, saving time.

There are disadvantages, too:

- Easy access may not be possible.
- There is less spontaneity,
- There are no clues to mood through tone or body language.
- The motivation to participate may be purely external: a course requirement, a higher grade.

The feedback to faculty from peers and students about the effectiveness of any teaching or learning activities can alert them to a thoroughgoing redesign of the course structure to eliminate any significant omissions or overkill in treating the topics. Some items could be combined, dropped, or replaced, making the work flow easier to handle for students or teachers. If changes are in order, the team must decide which elements to change first (Weimer, 1993).

Third, *if emotions of team members prevent objectivity in covering course content or assessing results, what advice could be had* from an outside consultant? An experienced expert? A generalist? A specialist? A student? An administrator? A teacher of education? An artist? A journalist? A psychologist? A management expert? An immigrant? A handicapped person? A poor person? Someone from another culture? Someone from the past or the future?

Careful review may lead to the conclusion that certain skills need to be added to the team. This could be done by adding more members, rotating personnel, or training the present team better. If the mix of teachers or students, with regard to, for example, age, gender, culture, or major field were modified, more might be done with fewer people or at lower cost. Replacing people with mechanical or automated equipment would have significant gains or losses too.

Fourth, *how can people be motivated to increase their productivity?* What do they want? Appreciation and encouragement from team members or management? More money? Release time? Better equipment? Better library support? Better rooms? Teaching aides? Workshops? Travel? Research grants?

Team responsibilities might be divided according to the team's skills, interests, and styles. Some may prefer to work alone. Some may like routine work without decision making. Some enjoy taking care of details. Some like to be in the spotlight, others to work behind the scenes. Some like to lead, others to follow. Thus, all contribute to the total team effort. Adapting tasks to people can reduce sources of friction and raise morale.

Failures are learning opportunities for both the students and the teachers. Perhaps their expectations were unrealistic. There may be some advantage to taking a whole new perspective in the evaluation, redefining a defeat as a victory, a weakness as a strength, a liability as an asset, or a disappointment as a blessing in disguise. Changing perspectives may be too daunting for a single teacher, but a team can encourage whole new ways of looking at a subject.

If notable weaknesses have emerged, it may be useful to develop a contingency plan in case they are repeated. The team should decide in advance on the danger signals to watch for and alternative lines of action to take if necessary.

CLASSROOM PERFORMANCE

As professionals, teachers must be constantly concerned about keeping current in their field and improving their performance. Student feedback is valuable, but students are not trained professionals, and their perspective is often skewed by self-interest. Self-observation is useful but often spotty. The most desirable observation of teaching comes from other teachers, who know what they are looking for.

Much of the observation of teaching that goes on within the team is informal. Teachers watch how others lecture, use props, and handle students. They see what is going on the minds of students and teacher in dialogue. The observers have their own point of view. Some may analyze teaching in terms of anxiety or control, others see it as a process of communication, and still others look at it as an artistic performance. All of these approaches are valid—and complementary. They can provide insightful feedback leading to improvement.

Formal observation involves measurement, using some instrument or set of criteria to focus on what to look and listen for and assigning quantitative values to the data—the more specific, the better. For example, it helps a teacher to know that in one class session 14 questions were asked to elicit facts, one to elicit an explanation or interpretation, and two to elicit values. This gives the teacher a snapshot of what was happening in this discussion period. The teacher, or team, then can ask whether the time might have been spent more profitably on valuative or interpretive questions.

One of the most effective ways to analyze and improve what actually takes place in the classroom is the *interaction analysis,* pioneered by Ned Flanders. A class session is taped. At 3- or 5-second intervals, the observer notes which of the following interactions is taking place, using the numbers of the categories listed below. The recorder then writes the numbers in columns to chart the picture of the entire class period.

- Teacher talk
    1. Accepts and clarifies positive and negative feelings
    2. Praises and encourages
    3. Accepts or uses student ideas
    4. Asks questions
    5. Lectures, giving facts or opinions
    6. Gives directions or orders
    7. Criticizes student behavior; justifies teacher behavior
- Student talk
    8. Student talk—response
    9. Student talk—initiation
- Silence
    10. Silence or confusion (Hyman, 1970, pp. 266-267)[2]

The great advantage of Flanders' interaction analysis is that the teacher can listen to a taped class, analyze it, diagnose problems, and prescribe remedies immediately. Using it can radically transform teacher behavior, provided that the teachers know that learning is in direct proportion to the active engagement of students in the learning process. The more active students are in class, the more they learn.

With practice, the types of teacher questions can be subdivided into those seeking facts, interpretations, or values. Also, student-to-student interactions can be charted to see if any individuals dominate the discussions.

Small-group discussions have all the dynamics of small groups, with talkative and shy personalities, struggles for power and attention, establishment of coalitions or cliques, and the testing of what behaviors will be permitted. Lest discussions get derailed onto sports and weather, teachers or discussion leaders must direct attention to the central points to be learned, model courtesy and respect for all, draw out the shy, and affirm contributions.

They must also develop skills in asking questions in such a way as to stimulate not just the memory but also the imagination of students. Ice-breakers can get a discussion going. Ask about feelings, not just facts. Ask about meanings when different facts are juxtaposed. Give a spot quiz, then have them share and critique their answers (Hyman, 1970, pp. 217-255; see also Cunningham, 1971).

IN-SERVICE PROGRAMS

In-service training programs can deliberately address weaknesses that surface in the postcourse assessments. Periodically, essential topics can be covered in workshops or monthly meetings:

- Philosophies of education
- Designing a program
- Choosing teaching styles
- Selecting team members
- Choosing the type of team
- Leadership issues
- Fields and subject matter to be studied
- Training and decision making
- Evaluation and improvement
- Resources needed
- Classroom interaction
- Use of resources and facilities
- Educational psychology
- Time and stress management
- Grading and discipline
- Communication and use of multimedia
- Creativity and self-expression
- Questioning skills in lectures and discussion groups
- Testing and evaluating

Administrators should be included in the in-service program so that they can hear firsthand the experiences and concerns of the teachers. It is good for them to share in the ongoing struggle for improvement. Their presence shows that they are convinced that learning is a lifelong project. Teachers must also see that administrators are not indifferent but ready to help insofar as they can.

The needs of teachers to experience the freedom to be creative have to be balanced with the support of a group. In-service training can serve these needs by scheduling lectures and discussions. Better still, it can use an inductive approach, centering on case studies that lead to the articulation of general principles, then to practical applications.

SUPPORT SYSTEMS

An abundance of resources—posters, maps, and charts; overhead projectors and overlays; educational television, videotapes, and audiotapes—can help teachers make class presentations more vivid and interesting.

Both lectures and discussions can be videotaped, then played back and studied for ways to improve. Actors and preachers do this, checking for gestures, articulation, tone, facial expression, and body movement. Teachers must pay attention to all of this, for the style of expression either helps the students understand and appreciate the content or gets in the way.

Use of teacher aides, like use of nursing aides and administrative aides, cuts costs and reduces time spent in nonteaching or supportive tasks. This frees teachers to prepare in more depth, to rethink approaches, and to interact more directly with students. Aides may be drawn from beginning teachers, retired teachers, parents interested but not credentialed, part-time teachers with other work (paraprofessionals), or clerical help.

Outside the classroom, computer-assisted instruction, including gaming, simulation, and the Internet, as well as teaching machines and programmed instruction, have long been used in science and language laboratories, industry, and the military services. In learning centers at universities, they have moved much of the drudgery of correcting grammar, punctuation, and spelling from teachers or tutors to machines that never tire nor grow impatient. Proceeding in small steps, with instant feedback, students learn at their own pace. They may even get impatient enough at their own repeated errors that they learn the right thing to do. Computer games have taught them to learn from mistakes.

NOTES

1. Particularly useful discussions of technology and faculty productivity can be found regularly in the journals *Syllabus, Technological Horizons in Education,* and *Imaging.*

2. Hyman (1970, pp. 266-267) presents a much more complicated instrument of his own design. This, too, can be fruitfully applied to team teaching once the team is familiar with Flanders. Another, less complicated variant of Flanders was developed by Amidon and Hunter (1966).

14

How to Support the Team

Support for the team can range from encouragement and recognition to providing buildings and equipment to make their jobs easier. Time and personnel issues can involve hidden costs. Attention will be given to all these issues.[1]

FINANCING

There will be some higher costs. Budgets must be adjusted for adequate classroom and media facilities and additional audiovisual materials. Library circulation increases. Television and videotapes will be used more frequently. Teacher aides or graduate students are usually hired to handle many details. They are often given teaching fellowships or paid an hourly salary with no benefits. Bonuses or release time may be given to team leaders. Other team members may be given release time or subsidies for workshops or seminars or travel connected to improving their teaching (see Bair & Woodard, 1964, pp. 177-187, for details).

What does one get for these higher costs? Higher-quality teaching and learning. If learning objectives are properly specified, evidence can be provided that students have learned with greater accuracy, understanding, satisfaction, and skill in application. Retention rates, acceptance of graduates by graduate schools and employers, and consequent recruitment of new students improve. If teaching objectives are also specified, the team can testify to greater enthusiasm, imagination, scholarship, and publications. Yes, there will be higher costs, but they will be worth it. The results should impress accreditation agencies.

In fact, all of this can be much less expensive than reducing the student-teacher ratio, and far more effective in raising the quality of teaching. Much of the costs can be recouped by tripling, quadrupling, or quintupling normal class size or large lectures. Large lectures are generally better organized and illustrated. Small-group discussions can be led either by faculty members of the team or by interns, graduate students, or teacher aides.

To cut costs even further, nonprofessional staff may take over some of the nonteaching responsibilities currently carried by faculty. Business and industry have long recognized the principle that no task should be assigned to a highly paid employee if it can be equally well performed by a less expensive employee. Universities could learn and apply that principle.

Part of the regular research and development budget may be allocated to orientation and training of the teams. Most of their ongoing formation can be handled through workshops open to all the faculty.

Computerizing the schedules for rooms, teachers, and students makes it possible to generate various alternative scenarios within the budget limits set by the dean or academic vice president.

PHYSICAL FACILITIES

Buildings ideally should be built with team teaching in mind. Flexibility enables the same space to be used for several purposes.

The greatest need is for well-designed large lecture halls seating 150 or more, with multilevel lighting. If these are created by opening folding or sliding doors, which can be closed to provide smaller rooms for discussion, so much the better.[2]

An alternative is a closed-circuit television system in which the same film or lecture is piped into several classrooms, providing something like the equivalent of a lecture hall but without the highly desirable interaction with all the students.

Desks and mobile chairs with writing platforms facilitate breaking large groups into small discussion sessions within the same room. But already-existing rooms can be adapted with some imagination. Noise can be modified with "white" background noise, carpeting, drapes, upholstery, and an acoustical ceiling and walls (see Bair & Woodward, 1964, pp. 36-60). Oddly shaped spaces can readily be used for small discussion groups. Good room design, sloped, with sound baffling, can achieve a feeling of intimacy even for groups as large as 100.

Thought should also be given to putting offices of team members in the same area, facilitating interaction outside class. The team could meet formally in a room otherwise designated for small-group discussions, or in a section of the teachers' lounge.

EQUIPMENT

A tape recorder is essential: All large-group presentations should be taped so that they can be reviewed by absentees and other students who find this a useful way to repeat the experience.

An overhead projector is essential for large groups because chalkboards cannot easily be read at a distance. A copier or printer capable of producing colored overlays must be available to the team in the office or duplicating center. For small groups, chalkboards can be simulated by flip charts or newsprint with markers.

A portable, battery-operated microphone is useful for guest lecturer or student use in large lecture halls.

Film and slide projectors complement television monitors on which videotapes or closed-circuit television can be shown.

Closed-circuit television, multiple copies of videotapes in separate classrooms, or even distance learning via video conferencing by fiber-optic telephone cable or satellite dishes or the Internet make it possible for many disparate groups of people to be taught simultaneously. Interaction can be enhanced by two-way video. This is seen regularly on television news programs and public television roundtable discussion groups, with various people interacting around the globe. The same can be done for academic learning.

All of this demands money: computers, video cameras, wiring, wide-screen monitors, lighting, soundproofing, technician and teacher salaries, Internet/satellite fees, advertising, insurance; library access for off-campus students.[3]

Not all learning takes place in the classroom. The chairs may all be in a circle, but in the electronic age, knowledge cannot be so easily surrounded and captured. It flows in a steady stream through modems into computers. There it is readily accessed by individuals—but they may be overwhelmed by the sheer mass of data. How can they screen, interpret, and organize it so that it makes sense?

In class, students learn how to put the technology at their service: how to formulate questions so that the data search is focused and fruitful. Lectures can address these skills generally; group discussions sharpen their talents. Then they polish their gifts through personal practice. Team teaching helps them by providing models of how scholars interact to improve the quality of questions, put the questions into the right order, and share the results.

Software programs can offer individuals the benefit of programmed instruction in science, computer, and language laboratories. These programs encourage active student engagement and learning, acceptance of personal responsibility, and the desire to achieve by association of the unfamiliar with the familiar, frequent repetition, movement from the simple to the complex, immediate rein-forcement or correction, and variable rates adapted to the learners. Many of them make learning fun. Such programs are used successfully in industry and the military services to teach information, hone skills, and form values (see Johnson & Hunt, 1968, pp. 137-142).

Widespread use of such materials in computer centers or at home can move repetitive drills out of the classroom and free students and teachers to concentrate on higher-order thinking: analysis, synthesis, creative hypothesis, judgment, and application. They can be used by absentees, by slower learners who profit from more repetition, and by advanced learners to move ahead of the class or to cover areas that would not be treated in class.

These programs can be used to introduce students to material before treatment in class, to review material after class, to teach a standard course in less time, or to teach more content in a standard length of time. They can be used in conjunction with team teaching to bring down costs.

Universities in the past have provided students with computer laboratories with built-in programs. As prices drop and hardware efficiency rises, more colleges are now requiring students to have at least a portable computer and to buy their own software, much as they buy expensive textbooks. This shifts the expenses from the universities to the students, but the hardware and software remain useful long after graduation.

TIME

Time will be needed by administrators for rescheduling faculty and rooms and for dealing with the personality problems and stress that the new system may bring for the team members. In practice, this should take no more time than is currently assigned to these tasks. A master schedule can be generated on the computer to reflect the needs of each faculty team for access to large lecture halls and small discussion space. If conflict among faculty does not arise from team teaching, it will arise from something else.

More important, the team must meet as a whole periodically to brainstorm, plan, assess, evaluate, and redesign. Lecturers need to write and rehearse, to research textual and audiovisual materials for incorporation into the lecture, and to get feedback from the team. Discussion leaders must develop questioning skills together before and after class. Some group meetings can be scheduled during summers or intersessions; others must take place during the semester or quarter. All of these must not interfere with mandatory general faculty meetings, department meetings, or committee meetings. Time is needed for each of these tasks and for generating a master schedule that makes the meetings possible. Well-run universities have a master calendar, planned at least 1 year ahead, into which other activities can be inserted.

Some thought must be given to variants. Should a team lecture precede or follow an individual basic lecture? Should it precede or follow discussion groups, or should it do both, introducing and recapping material? Office hours must be provided for students to contact faculty outside class. All of this input should be fed to the administrative staff responsible for the college schedule. To meet all these needs, release time may have to be given to team members.

PERSONNEL

Assistant and associate deans have different areas of expertise and responsibility. Most of them want to provide time, funds, and encouragement for projects. Just explaining an idea to them may help pieces fall into place. Some of them may have experience in team teaching themselves and can make useful and creative suggestions.

Most universities have centers that provide a broad spectrum of services: psychological counseling, career counseling, assistance with health, assistance with learning difficulties, and assistance with computers technology, and instructional media. Students and faculty should work with the people at the centers to profit from their input. For example, the staff of the duplicating center need sufficient notice to get the job done. People at instructional media appreciate advance requests for hardware or software so that potential scheduling conflicts are avoided.

Secretaries and teacher aides provide incalculable help. The more they understand of what the team is trying to do and the methods employed, the more focused and valuable will be their support.

Librarians provide essential help. They order and process materials needed. More important, they can suggest bibliographical resources in print and other media. The team should meet with them to profit from their suggestions in the planning and evaluation process. They may also be able to make multiple copies of certain materials available to students through a reserve room.

NOTES

1. Extensive treatment of this subject from the viewpoint of an administrator is given in Trusty (1964).

2. Useful diagrams are provided in Hanslovsky et al. (1969, pp. 20-23). An entire chapter is devoted to building design, complete with diagrams, in LaFauci and Richter (1970, pp. 82-111).

3. Particularly useful discussions of technology and faculty productivity can be found regularly in the journals *Syllabus, Technological Horizons in Education,* and *Imaging.*

15

Common Problems
and Potentials

Looking back on this treatment of team teaching, what general conclusions emerge?

- It has been going on a long time, for thousands of years, in formal and informal settings. In this century, it has been used successfully on all levels of formal education, as well as in business, medicine, and military services.
- It works with all kinds of students in all kinds of settings: large groups, small groups, and individuals.
- It has been used within a single discipline or cutting across several fields. The richer the mix of ideas and personalities, the greater the stimulation for both teachers and students.
- The teams can be organized vertically (hierarchically) or horizontally (democratically), but whatever the organizational structures, attention must be paid to issues of conflict and leadership so that the team works smoothly.
- The key questions deal with setting goals and objectives, choosing the members, training the team, designing a program, making decisions together, evaluating the results, and redesigning to do better.
- To operate effectively, the team needs support: encouragement, facilities, equipment, time, and personnel.
- The chief benefit of team teaching is to improve the quality of education, helping the teachers teach better and helping the students learn better.

POTENTIALS

The quality of lectures improves. Faced with the prospect of addressing a large group in the presence of one or more colleagues, teachers prepare more thoroughly. The lecture tends to be more interesting, better organized, faster paced, and with more content. Aware of the learning objectives agreed upon by the team, the lecturer presents an overview of the key ideas from the background reading; analyzes, illustrates, clarifies, reinforces the central content; invites questions and comments; and finally summarizes and applies the material. Other team members cut in from time to time to raise questions or propose alternate interpretations, provoking the students to think for themselves and engage more actively in the class. The entire period is more lively, more free-flowing, and more creative—for teachers and students. Because the presentation is taped, it may be reviewed later by students and evaluated critically by the team.

From these superior lectures, students get a more comprehensive view of the whole before exploring individual parts. The structure makes it easier to shape skills in critical thinking. Students get a sense of closure from the summary. Their curiosity is aroused. Connections with other fields and current events are indicated as avenues for research. Research tools are suggested. Scholarly attitudes and behavior are modeled by the team.

The quality of discussions also improves. Key points of the lecture are clarified, enriched, reinforced, and tied in to practical applications and skills. The abstract is made concrete. Or better, out of concrete examples the students derive the underlying principles. The students form a lifelong habit: observe–judge–act.

Reactions of students—confusion, anger, enthusiasm—become more apparent. This makes it easier to get them involved. All are encouraged to participate actively and listen attentively. As a result, self-expression becomes more comfortable, more logical, more responsible, and more respectful of the dignity and viewpoints of others (Casey, 1964, pp. 170-176).

The exchange of scholarly insights inside and outside class is intellectually exciting to both teachers and students. New research projects arise. Boredom vanishes (Weimer, 1993).

PROBLEMS

Problems will surely arise. Anxieties about risks are part of all significant change. Administrators will worry about costs. Those enamored of structural rigidity will oppose any change, but especially one that threatens a loss of control through decentralized decision making.[1]

Scholars will be concerned with possible tensions between their teaching and research. Those on interdisciplinary teams will particularly feel a strain in developing a broad knowledge of the principles, content, and methodologies of other academic areas outside their own field of expertise (Antczak, 1994; Kriege, 1973; Nicodemus, 1992).

No matter how dedicated the teachers, they will want to know how their workload and salary will be affected.

It is not easy for seasoned teachers to surrender autonomy to a group. It is hard to take—and give—criticism to peers. Personality conflicts are intensified by frequent interaction.

Team teaching also demands time and energy in the planning and evaluation sessions. It cannot work easily with a part-time faculty. Patience is strained by the slowness of collective decision making. It takes longer to agree on the learning and teaching outcomes, the required and recommended reading, the list and sequence of topics on the syllabus, the type and frequency of tests, the norms of grading, and the mix of lecture, discussion, and independent study.

Students will welcome the variety of voices and viewpoints. But they will fail to see the connections between disciplines and the value of comparing different points of view to develop critical thinking skills unless these are explicitly pointed out to them by the team, and frequently.

Many of these problems are interrelated. Taken together, they may seem formidable, even overwhelming. But they are not insurmountable. Faculty at other universities have faced these problems and solved them. One can learn from others' mistakes and successes.

More important, these problems open the door to adventure. The Chinese character for crisis, *wei-chi,* is made up of two characters, "danger" and "opportunity" (Gmelch, 1993, p. 4).

Much of the personal growth of team members comes out of the challenges these problems present. As issues are raised, discussed, and thought through and as tentative solutions are tried out and evaluated, the whole process of teaching moves onto a higher level of sophistication. In the long run, this is deeply satisfying to the faculty. Their self-confidence is more deeply rooted. Their readiness to consult and collaborate is more mature.

Team teaching brings higher education into line with broad cultural movements from unbridled individualism to teamwork. Teachers now expect this in industry, politics, and scientific research and are familiar with its widespread use in academic committees. Certain issues, such as racism, peace, gender issues, poverty, urbanization, and ecology, defy traditional single-discipline analysis. An interrelated reality demands multifaceted analysis.

What's more, technological developments and dropping costs virtually ensure some sort of team teaching using distance learning together with site visits in the new century.[2]

The future has already begun.

NOTES

1. LaFauci and Richter (1970, pp. 113-123) presented a thoughtful and balanced weighing of the limitations and potentials of team teaching.

2. LaFauci and Richter (1970, pp. 127-135) presented a fascinating array of imaginative scenarios for team teaching in the future. See also Showers and Joyce (1996, pp. 12-17).

References

Amidon, E., & Hunter, E. (1966). *Improving teaching: The analysis of classroom verbal interaction.* New York: Holt, Rinehart & Winston.

Angelo, T. A., & Cross, K. P. (1993). *Classroom assessment techniques: A handbook for college teachers.* San Francisco: Jossey-Bass.

Antczak, F. (1994). *Learning and the public research university: 22 suggestions to reduce tensions between teaching and research.* East Lansing, MI: National Center for Research on Teacher Learning. (ERIC Document Reproduction Service No. ED372689)

Arkin, A. (1996, January 19). The triumph of Mr (or Ms) Motivator. *Times Educational Supplement,* p. 9B.

Bair, M., & Woodward, R. G. (1964). *Team teaching in action.* Boston: Houghton-Mifflin.

Barnard, C. I. (1938). *The functions of the executive.* Cambridge, MA: Harvard University Press.

Beggs, D. W., III. (1964a). Fundamental considerations for team teaching. In D. W. Beggs, III (Ed.), *Team teaching: Bold new venture* (pp. 29-50). Bloomington: Indiana University Press.

Beggs, D. W., III. (Ed.). (1964b). *Team teaching: Bold new venture.* Bloomington: Indiana University Press.

Buckley, F. J. (1976). Improving college students' religious attitudes and values. *Lumen Vitae, 31,* 455-462.

Casey, V. M. (1964). A summary of team teaching: Its patterns and potentials. In D. W. Beggs, III (Ed.), *Team teaching: Bold new venture* (pp. 164-178). Bloomington: Indiana University Press.

Chamberlin, L. J. (1969). *Team teaching: Organization and administration.* Columbus, OH: Merrill.

Covey, S. (1991). *Principle-centered leadership.* New York: Summit.

Cunningham, R. T. (1971). Developing question-asking skills. In J. Weigand (Ed.), *Developing teacher competencies* (pp. 81-130). Englewood Cliffs, NJ: Prentice Hall.

Davis, H. S. (1966). *How to organize an effective team teaching program.* Englewood Cliffs, NJ: Prentice Hall.

Esterby-Smith, M. (1984). Making management education more student-centered. *Management Education and Development, 15,* 221-236.

Gardner, J. W. (1968). *No easy victories.* New York: Harper & Row.

Garmston, R. (1987). How administrators support peer coaching. *Educational Leadership, 44*(5), 18-26.

Garmston, R., Lindner, C., & Whitaker, J. (1993). Reflections on cognitive coaching. *Educational Leadership, 51*(2), 57-61.

Gmelch, W. H. (1993). *Coping with faculty stress.* Thousand Oaks, CA: Sage.

Hanslovsky, G., Moyer, S., & Wagner, H. (1969). *Why team teaching?* Columbus, OH: Charles E. Merrill.

Havas, E. (1994). Modeling diversity in the classroom. *Equity and Excellence in Education, 27*(3), 43-47.

Heller, M. P. (1964). Qualities for team members. In D. W. Beggs, III (Ed.), *Team teaching: Bold new venture* (pp. 145-154). Bloomington: Indiana University Press.

Hyman, R. T. (1970). *Ways of teaching.* Philadelphia: J. B. Lippincott.

Johnson, R. H., Jr., & Hunt, J. J. (1968). *Rx for team teaching.* Minneapolis, MN: Burgess.

Jones, R. W. (1964). Procedures for inaugurating team teaching. In D. W. Beggs, III (Ed.), *Team teaching: Bold new venture* (pp. 92-103). Bloomington: Indiana University Press.

Kriege, J. (1973). Limitations on paired-associate teaching teams. *California Journal of Educational Research, 24*(1), 23-27.

Kruger, L. J., Struzziero, J., Watts, R., & Vacca, D. (1995). The relationship between organizational support and satisfaction with teacher assistance teams. *Remedial and Special Education, 16,* 203-211.

LaFauci, H. M., & Richter, P. E. (1970). *Team teaching at the college level.* New York: Pergamon.

Mead, M. (1958, November-December). Thinking ahead: Why is education obsolete? *Harvard Business Review, 36,*23-30.

Neubert, G. A., & Bratton, E. C. (1987). Team coaching: Staff development side by side. *Educational Leadership, 44*(5), 29-33.

Nicodemus, R. (1992). *Course teams.* East Lansing, MI: National Center for Research on Teacher Learning. (ERIC Document Reproduction Service No. ED346798)

Olivero, J. L. (1964). Evaluation considerations for team teaching. In D. W. Beggs, III (Ed.), *Team teaching: Bold new venture* (pp. 104-117). Bloomington: Indiana University Press.

Showers, B. (1982). *Transfer of training: The contribution of coaching.* Eugene, OR: Center for Educational Policy and Management.

Showers, B. (1984). *Peer coaching: A strategy for facilitating transfer of training.* Eugene, OR: Center for Educational Policy and Management.

Showers, B., & Joyce, B. (1996). The evolution of peer coaching. *Educational Leadership, 53*(6), 12-17.

Singer, I. J. (1964). What team teaching really is. In D. W. Beggs, III (Ed.), *Team teaching: Bold new venture* (pp. 13-22). Bloomington: Indiana University Press.

Sofield, L. (1995). *The collaborative leader.* Notre Dame, IN: Ave Maria.

Tomchek, D. (1964). A teacher comments on team teaching. In D. W. Beggs, III (Ed.), *Team teaching: Bold new venture* (pp. 118-130). Bloomington: Indiana University Press.

Trusty, F. M. (1964). An administrator looks at team teaching. In D. W. Beggs, III (Ed.), *Team teaching: Bold new venture* (pp. 131-144). Bloomington: Indiana University Press.

Weimer, M. (1993). *Improving your classroom teaching.* Thousand Oaks, CA: Sage.

Wills, L. K, (1964). Team teaching in the content fields. In D. W. Beggs, III (Ed.), *Team teaching: Bold new venture* (pp. 155-163). Bloomington: Indiana University Press.

Bibliography

Chapter 1

Anderson, R. H. (1989). A second wave of interest in team teaching. *Education Digest, 54*(6), 18-21.

Bair, M., & Woodward, R. G. (1964). *Team teaching in action.* Boston: Houghton-Mifflin.

Beggs, D. W., III. (Ed.). (1964). *Team teaching: Bold new venture.* Bloomington: Indiana University Press.

Bergen, D. (1994). Developing the art and science of team teaching. *Childhood Education, 70,* 242-243.

Castle, E. B. (1970). *The teacher.* London: Oxford University Press.

Chamberlin, L. J. (1969). *Team teaching: Organization and administration.* Columbus, OH: Merrill.

Davis, H. S. (1966). *How to organize an effective team teaching program.* Englewood Cliffs, NJ: Prentice Hall.

Gage, N. L. (1963). *Handbook of research on teaching.* Chicago: Rand-McNally.

Garmston, R. (1987). How administrators support peer coaching. *Educational Leadership, 44*(5), 18-26.

Garmston, R., Lindner, C., & Whitaker, J. (1993). Reflections on cognitive coaching. *Educational Leadership, 51*(2), 57-61.

Hyman, R. T. (1970). *Ways of teaching.* Philadelphia: J. B. Lippincott.

Johnson, R. H., Jr., & Hunt, J. J. (1968). *Rx for team teaching.* Minneapolis, MN: Burgess.

Katz, J. (1993). *Turning professors into teachers: A new approach to faculty development and student learning.* Phoenix, AZ: Oryx.

LaFauci, H. M., & Richter, P. E. (1970). *Team teaching at the college level.* New York: Pergamon.

Marrou, H. I. (1956). *A history of education in antiquity.* New York: Sheed & Ward.

McCormick, P. J., & Cassidy, F. P. (1957). *History of education.* Washington, DC: Catholic Education Press.

Miller, J. (1995). Battle hymn of American studies: Team teaching. *English Journal, 84*(1), 88-93.

Morsink, C. V., Thomas, C. C., & Correa, V. (1991). *Interactive teaming.* New York: Macmillan.

Mulhern, J. (1959). *History of education.* New York: Ronald.

Neubert, G. A., & Bratton, E. C. (1987). Team coaching: Staff development side by side. *Educational Leadership, 44*(5), 29-33.

Power, E. J. (1970). *Main currents in the history of education* (2nd ed.). New York: McGraw-Hill.

Prichard, K. W., & Sawyer, R. M. (Eds.). (1994). *Handbook of college teaching: Theory and applications.* Westport, CT: Greenwood.

Showers, B. (1982). *Transfer of training: The contribution of coaching.* Eugene, OR: Center for Educational Policy and Management.

Showers, B. (1984). *Peer coaching: A strategy for facilitating transfer of training.* Eugene, OR: Center for Educational Policy and Management.

Showers, B., & Joyce, B. (1996). The evolution of peer coaching. *Educational Leadership, 53*(6), 12-17.

Singer, I. J. (1964). What team teaching really is. In D. W. Beggs, III (Ed.), *Team teaching: Bold new venture* (pp. 13-22). Bloomington: Indiana University Press. This book has several useful graphs and case studies.

Ulich, R. (1954). *Three thousand years of educational wisdom* (2nd ed.). Cambridge, MA: Harvard University Press.

Chapter 2

Antczak, F. (1994). *Learning and the public research university: 22 suggestions to reduce tensions between teaching and research.* East Lansing, MI: National Center for Research on Teacher Learning. (ERIC Document Reproduction Service No. ED372689)

Arkin, A. (1996, January 19). The triumph of Mr (or Ms) Motivator. *Times Educational Supplement,* p. 9B.

Bair, M., & Woodward, R. G. (1964). *Team teaching in action.* Boston: Houghton-Mifflin.

Beggs, D. W., III. (Ed.). (1964). *Team teaching: Bold new venture.* Bloomington: Indiana University Press.

Bergman, F. (1990). Tandem teaching relieves boredom, maximizes class time. *NASSP Bulletin, 74,* 89-94.

Chamberlin, L. J. (1969). *Team teaching: Organization and administration.* Columbus, OH: Merrill.

Collison, M. (1993, November 10). Learning communities. *Chronicle of Higher Education,* p. A30.

Flanagan, M. F., & Ralston, D. A. (1983). Intra-coordinated team teaching: Benefits for both students and instructors, *Teaching of Psychology, 10*(2), 116-117.

Frey, J. D., & Nowaczyk, R. H. (1982). Combining research interests with the teaching of undergraduates: A report on a team-taught seminar. *Teaching of Psychology, 9,* 220-221.

Hanslovsky, G., Moyer, S., & Wagner, H. (1969). *Why team teaching?* Columbus, OH: Charles E. Merrill.

Johnson, R. H., Jr., & Hunt, J. J. (1968). *Rx for team teaching.* Minneapolis, MN: Burgess.

Kaikai, S. M., & Kaikai, R. E. (1990). *Positive ways to avoid instructor burnout.* East Lansing, MI: National Center for Research on Teacher Learning. (ERIC Document Reproduction Service No. ED320623)

Kaplan, R. (1974). The scientist/professor and undergraduate education. *Teaching of Psychology, 1*(1), 24-27.

Kirschenbaum, D. S., & Riechmann, S. W. (1975). Learning with gusto in introductory psychology. *Teaching of Psychology, 2*(2), 72-76.

LaFauci, H. M., & Richter, P. E. (1970). *Team teaching at the college level.* New York: Pergamon.

McIntosh, B., & Shipman, H. (1996). The power of collaboration: Peer collaboration—a powerful mechanism for effecting change in science education. *Journal of College Science Teaching, 25,* 364-365.

Mead, M. (1958, November-December). Thinking ahead: Why is education obsolete? *Harvard Business Review, 36,*23-30.

Meyer, J. (1994). *Teaching through teams in communication courses: Letting structuration happen.* East Lansing, MI: National Center for Research on Teacher Learning. (ERIC Document Reproduction Service No. ED381816)

Miller, J. (1995). Battle hymn of American studies: Team teaching. *English Journal, 84*(1), 88-93.

Parson, S. R. (1994). Program development, team instruction, and impact on faculty, 1994. *NASSP Bulletin, 78*(559), 62-64.

Roberts, H., Gonzales, J. C., Lou, R., Scott, O. L., Johns, A. M., Harris, O. D., & Huff, D. J. (1994). *Teaching from a multicultural perspective.* Thousand Oaks, CA: Sage.

Seal, R. K. (1993, Fall). Resources for developing senior faculty as teachers. *New Directions for Teaching and Learning, 55,* 99-111.

Showers, B. (1980). Improving inservice training: The messages of research. *Educational Leadership, 37,* 379-385.

Showers, B. (1982). *Transfer of training: The contribution of coaching.* Eugene, OR: Center for Educational Policy and Management.

Showers, B. (1984). *Peer coaching: A strategy for facilitating transfer of training.* Eugene, OR: Center for Educational Policy and Management.

Showers, B. (1995). *Student achievement through staff development: Fundamentals of school renewal.* White Plains, NY: Longman.

Showers, B., & Joyce, B. (1996). The evolution of peer coaching. *Educational Leadership, 53*(6), 12-17.

Swick, K. J., & Hanley, P. E. (1980). *Stress and the classroom teacher: What research says to the teacher.* Washington, DC: National Education Association.

Toomey, B. G., & Eldridge, W. D. (1982). The interactive team: A non-sexist teaching approach. *College Student Journal, 16*(1), 4-8.

Ware, M. E., Gardner, L. E., & Murphy, D. P. (1978). Team teaching introductory psychology, *Teaching of Psychology, 5*(3), 127-130.

Weimer, M. (1993). *Improving your classroom teaching.* Thousand Oaks, CA: Sage.

Chapter 3

Adams, D. M. (1990). *Cooperative learning and educational media: Collaborating with technology and each other.* Englewood Cliffs, NJ: Educational Technology Publications.

Beggs, D. W., III. (Ed.). (1964). *Team teaching: Bold new venture.* Bloomington: Indiana University Press.

Bess, J. S. (Ed.). (1997). *Teaching well and liking it: Motivating faculty to teach effectively.* Baltimore: Johns Hopkins University Press.

Bruffee, K. A. (1993). *Collaborative learning: Higher education, interdependence, and the authority of knowledge.* Baltimore: Johns Hopkins University Press.

Chamberlin, L. J. (1969). *Team teaching: Organization and administration.* Columbus, OH: Merrill.

Davis, B. G. (1993). *Tools for teaching.* San Francisco: Jossey-Bass.

Davis, H. S. (1966). *How to organize an effective team teaching program.* Englewood Cliffs, NJ: Prentice Hall.

Eble, K. E. (1988). *The craft of teaching: A guide to mastering the professor's art.* San Francisco: Jossey-Bass.

Jacobs, H. H. (Ed.). (1989). *Interdisciplinary curriculum: Design and implementation.* Alexandria, VA: Association for Supervision and Curriculum Development.

Johnson, D. W., Johnson, R. T., & Smith, K. A. (1991). *Cooperative learning: Increasing college faculty instructional productivity.* Washington, DC: George Washington University, School of Education and Human Development.

Johnson, R. H., Jr., & Hunt, J. J. (1968). *Rx for team teaching.* Minneapolis, MN: Burgess.

Katz, J. (1993). *Turning professors into teachers: A new approach to faculty development and student learning.* Phoenix, AZ: Oryx.

Kriege, J. W. (1973). Limitations on paired-associate teaching teams. *California Journal of Educational Research, 24*(1), 23-27.

Lowman, J. (1984). *Mastering the techniques of teaching.* San Francisco: Jossey-Bass.

Maeroff, G. I. (1993). *Team building for school change.* New York: Teachers College Press.

Nolan, R. R. (1976). *How to succeed in team teaching—by really trying.* Palo Alto, CA: Stanford Center for Research and Development in Teaching.

Raker, R. (1994). *Integrated block scheduling and team teaching: 8 suggestions for better team teaching.* East Lansing, MI: National Center for Research on Teacher Learning. (ERIC Document Reproduction Service No. ED375667)

Tiberius, R. G. (1990). *Small group teaching.* Toronto: Ontario Institute for Studies in Education Press.

Weimer, M. (1993). *Improving your classroom teaching.* Thousand Oaks, CA: Sage.

Chapter 4

Bernhardt, K. L. (1964). *Discipline and child guidance.* New York: McGraw-Hill.

Bouton, C., & Garth, R. Y. (Eds.). (1983). *Learning in groups.* San Francisco: Jossey-Bass.

Chamberlin, L. J. (1969). *Team teaching: Organization and administration.* Columbus, OH: Merrill.

Davis, B. G. (1993). *Tools for teaching.* San Francisco: Jossey-Bass.

Davis, H. S. (1966). *How to organize an effective team teaching program.* Englewood Cliffs, NJ: Prentice Hall.

Matthews, A. (1997). *Bright college years: Inside the American campus today.* New York: Simon & Schuster.

Ramsey, G., & Silvia, A. (1993). Breaking barriers: Can student journalists and economists learn together? *College Teaching, 41*(4), 129-133.

Ross, R., & Stokes, C. S. (1984). *Implications and strategies for instruction of the nontraditional student in the conventional basic speech communication course.* East Lansing, MI: National Center for Research on Teacher Learning. (ERIC Document Reproduction Service No. ED250741)

Sacks, P. (1996). *Generation X goes to college.* Chicago: Open Court.

Schoem, D. (Ed.). (1993). *Multicultural teaching in the university.* Westport, CT: Praeger.

Slavin, R. E. (1991). *Student team learning: A practical guide to cooperative learning.* Washington, DC: National Education Association.

Webster, S. W. (1968). *Discipline in the classroom.* Chicago: Chandler.

Chapter 5

Beggs, D. W., III. (Ed.). (1964). *Team teaching: Bold new venture.* Bloomington: Indiana University Press.

Boice, R. (1992). *The new faculty member: Supporting and fostering professional development.* San Francisco: Jossey-Bass.

Cardozier, V. R. (1993). *Important lessons from innovative colleges and universities.* San Francisco: Jossey-Bass.

Davis, B. G. (1993). *Tools for teaching.* San Francisco: Jossey-Bass.

Drake, S. M. (1993). *Planning integrated curriculum: The call to adventure.* Alexandria, VA: Association for Supervision and Curriculum Development.

Esterby-Smith, M. (1984). Making management education more student-centered. *Management Education and Development, 15,* 221-236.

Hallinger, P., Leithwood, K., & Murphy, J. (Eds.). (1993). *Cognitive perspectives on educational leadership.* New York: Teachers College Press.

Hanslovsky, G., Moyer, S., & Wagner, H. (1969). *Why team teaching?* Columbus, OH: Charles E. Merrill.

Havas, E. (1994). Modeling diversity in the classroom. *Equity and Excellence in Education, 27*(3), 43-47.

Johnson, R. H., Jr., & Hunt, J. J. (1968). *Rx for team teaching.* Minneapolis, MN: Burgess.

Joyce, B. R. (1996). *Models of teaching.* Boston: Allyn & Bacon.

LaFauci, H. M., & Richter, P. E. (1970). *Team teaching at the college level.* New York: Pergamon.

Maeroff, G. I. (1993). *Team building for school change.* New York: Teachers College Press.

Matthews, A. (1997). *Bright college years: Inside the American campus today.* New York: Simon & Schuster.

McKeachie, W. J. (1994). *Teaching tips: Strategies, research, and theory for college and university teachers.* Lexington, MA: D. C. Heath.

Chapter 6

Beggs, D. W., III. (Ed.). (1964). *Team teaching: Bold new venture.* Bloomington: Indiana University Press.

Chamberlin, L. J. (1969). *Team teaching: Organization and administration.* Columbus, OH: Merrill.

Davis, H. S. (1966). *How to organize an effective team teaching program.* Englewood Cliffs, NJ: Prentice Hall.

Esterby-Smith, M., & Olve, N. G. (1984). Team teaching: Making management education more student-centered? *Management Education and Development, 15,* 221-236.

Garmston, R. (1987). How administrators support peer coaching. *Educational Leadership, 44*(5), 18-26.

Garmston, R., Lindner, C., & Whitaker, J. (1993). Reflections on cognitive coaching. *Educational Leadership, 51*(2), 57-61.

Hanslovsky, G., Moyer, S., & Wagner, H. (1969). *Why team teaching?* Columbus, OH: Charles E. Merrill.

Kent, K. M. (1985). A successful program of teachers assisting teachers. *Educational Leadership, 43*(3), 30-33.

LaFauci, H. M., & Richter, P. E. (1970). *Team teaching at the college level.* New York: Pergamon. Successful case studies abound.

Maeroff, G. I. (1993). *Team building for school change.* New York: Teachers College Press.

McIntosh, M. E., & Johnson, D. L. (1994). An instrument to facilitate communication between prospective team teachers. *Clearing House, 67,* 152-154.

Neubert, G. A., & Bratton, E. C. (1987). Team coaching: Staff development side by side. *Educational Leadership, 44*(5), 29-33.

Raywid, M. A. (1993). Finding time for collaboration. *Educational Leadership, 51*(1), 30-35.

Singer, I. J. (1964). What team teaching really is. In D. W. Beggs, III (Ed.), *Team teaching: Bold new venture* (pp. 13-22). Bloomington: Indiana University Press. This book has several useful graphs and case studies.

Chapter 7

Altshuler, K. (1991). The interdisciplinary classroom. *Physics Teacher, 29,* 428-429.

Andersen, L. R. (1991). *Improve the quality of instruction through interdisciplinary internationally oriented faculty resource teams.* East Lansing, MI: National Center for Research on Teacher Learning. (ERIC Document Reproduction Service No. ED369309)

Buckley, F. J. (1976). Improving college students' religious attitudes and values. *Lumen Vitae, 31,* 455-462.

Castro, R. M. (1993). Defining, supporting, and maintaining interprofessional education. *Journal of Educational Policy, 8*(5-6), 153-155.

Chandler, J. K., Davidson, A. I., & Harootunian, H. D. (Eds.). (1994). *Questions of evidence: Proof, practice, and persuasion across the disciplines.* Chicago: University of Chicago Press.

Clapsaddle, J., & Thomas, J. (1991). A healthy start for team teaching. *Vocational Education Journal, 66*(5), 28-29.

Clark, L., Gonzales, J. C., Lou, R., Scott, O. L., Johns, A. M., Harris, O. D., & Huff, D. J. (1992). *Project 30 and the pedagogy seminars: A report.* East Lansing, MI: National Center for Research on Teacher Learning. (ERIC Document Reproduction Service No. ED368687)

Hanslovsky, G., Moyer, S., & Wagner, H. (1969). *Why team teaching?* Columbus, OH: Charles E. Merrill.

Hussman, L. (1991, Fall). The faculty's forte: Team teaching the literature survey. *ADE Bulletin, 99,* 29-33.

Jacobs, H. H. (Ed.). (1989). *Interdisciplinary curriculum: Design and implementation.* Alexandria, VA: Association for Supervision and Curriculum Development.

Keeton, R. E., & Levy, R. J. (Eds.). (1996). *Team-teaching of substantive law and practice skills in substantive law contexts.* Chicago: American Bar Association.

LaFauci, H. M., & Richter, P. E. (1970). *Team teaching at the college level.* New York: Pergamon.

McIntosh, B., & Shipman, H. (1996). The power of collaboration: Peer collaboration—a powerful mechanism for effecting change in science education. *Journal of College Science Teaching, 25,* 364-365.

McLeod, S. H., & Soven, M. (Eds.). (1992). *Writing across the curriculum: A guide to developing programs.* Thousand Oaks, CA: Sage.

Meyer, J. (1994). *Teaching through teams in communication courses.* East Lansing, MI: National Center for Research on Teacher Learning. (ERIC Document Reproduction Service No. ED381816)

Miller, J. (1995). Battle hymn of American studies: Team teaching. *English Journal, 84*(1), 88-93.

Perry, L. A. M. (1993). *When experiential teaching is an experience.* East Lansing, MI: National Center for Research on Teacher Learning. (ERIC Document Reproduction Service No. ED368609)

Ramsey, G., & Silvia, A. (1993). Breaking barriers: Can student journalists and economists learn together? *College Teaching, 41*(4), 129-133.

Saccoman, J. T. (1996). Sabermetrics: The team teaching approach. *Education, 117,* 200-201.

Singer, I. J. (1964). What team teaching really is. In D. W. Beggs, III (Ed.), *Team teaching: Bold new venture* (pp. 16-22). Bloomington: Indiana University Press. This book has several useful graphs and case studies.

Walsh, W. B., Smith, G. L., & London, M. (1975). Developing an interface between engineering and the social sciences: An interdisciplinary team approach to solving societal problems, *American Psychologist, 30,* 1067-1071.

Waterbury, R. (1993). World studies at Queens College, CUNY. *Social Studies, 84*(2), 54-57.

Williams, K. G., & Kolupke, J. (1986). Psychology and literature: An interdisciplinary approach to the liberal curriculum. *Teaching of Psychology, 13*(2), 59-61.

Wills, L. K. (1964). Team teaching in the content fields. In D. W. Beggs, III (Ed.), *Team teaching: Bold new venture* (pp. 155-163). Bloomington: Indiana University Press.

Chapter 8

Beggs, D. W., III. (Ed.). (1964). *Team teaching: Bold new venture.* Bloomington: Indiana University Press. This book has several useful graphs and case studies.

Bennis, W. G. (1985). *Leaders: The strategies for taking charge.* New York: Harper & Row.

Bennis, W. G. (1989). *On becoming a leader.* Reading, MA: Addison-Wesley.

Bennis, W. G. (1993). *An invented life: Reflections on leadership and change.* Reading, MA: Addison-Wesley.

Bess, J. S. (Ed.). (1997). *Teaching well and liking it: Motivating faculty to teach effectively.* Baltimore: Johns Hopkins University Press.

Boles, K., & Troen, V. (1994). *Teacher leadership in a professional development school.* East Lansing, MI: National Center for Research on Teacher Learning. (ERIC Document Reproduction Service No. ED375103)

Bruffee, K. A. (1993). *Collaborative learning: Higher education, interdependence, and the authority of knowledge.* Baltimore: Johns Hopkins University Press.

Clark, S. (1972). *Building Christian community.* Notre Dame, IN: Ave Maria.

Covey, S. (1989). *The seven habits of highly effective people.* New York: Simon & Schuster.

Covey, S. (1991). *Principle-centered leadership.* New York: Summit.

Gardner, J. W. (1968). *No easy victories.* New York: Harper & Row.

Gardner, J. W. (1990). *On leadership.* New York: Free Press.

Hanslovsky, G., Moyer, S., & Wagner, H. (1969). *Why team teaching?* Columbus, OH: Charles E. Merrill.

Heifetz, R. A. (1994). *Leadership without easy answers.* Cambridge, MA: Belknap.

Katz, J. (1993). *Turning professors into teachers: A new approach to faculty development and student learning.* Phoenix, AZ: Oryx.

LaFauci, H. M., & Richter, P. E. (1970). *Team teaching at the college level.* New York: Pergamon.

Likert, R., & Likert, J. (1976). *New ways of managing conflict.* New York: McGraw-Hill.

Maeroff, G. I. (1993). *Team building for school change.* New York: Teachers College Press.

McClelland, D. C. (1984). *Motives, personality, and society.* New York: Praeger.

Ouchi, W. (1981). *Theory Z.* Reading, MA: Addison-Wesley.

Pellicer, L. (1995). *Handbook for teacher leaders.* Thousand Oaks, CA: Sage.

Saxe, S. (1986). *The effect of peer interaction and incentive on adult learner achievement.* San Francisco: University of San Francisco, School of Education.

Schmidt, W. H., & Buchanan, P. C. (1954). *Techniques that produce teamwork.* New London, CT: Arthur C. Croft.

Sofield, L. (1995). *The collaborative leader.* Notre Dame, IN: Ave Maria.

Tannenbaum, R., & Massarik, F. (1950). Participation by subordinates in the managerial decision-making process. *Canadian Journal of Economics and Political Science, 16,* 413-418.

Chapter 9

Austin, A. E., & Baldwin, R. G. (1992). *Faculty collaboration: Enhancing the quality of scholarship and teaching.* East Lansing, MI: National Center for Research on Teacher Learning. (ERIC Document Reproduction Service No. ED347958)

Brookfield, S. (1990). *The skillful teacher: On technique, trust, and responsiveness in the classroom.* San Francisco: Jossey-Bass.

Cardozier, V. R. (1993). *Important lessons from innovative colleges and universities.* San Francisco: Jossey-Bass.

Garmston, R. (1987). How administrators support peer coaching. *Educational Leadership, 44*(5), 18-26.

Garmston, R., Lindner, C., & Whitaker, J. (1993). Reflections on cognitive coaching. *Educational Leadership, 51*(2), 57-61.

Gmelch, W. H. (1993). *Coping with faculty stress.* Thousand Oaks, CA: Sage.

Hallinger, P., Leithwood, K., & Murphy, J. (Eds.). (1993). *Cognitive perspectives on educational leadership.* New York: Teachers College Press.

Joyce, B. R., Brown, C. C., Peck, L., & Butler, L. (Eds.). (1981). *Flexibility in teaching: An excursion into the nature of teaching and training.* New York: Longman.

Maeroff, G. I. (1993). *Team building for school change.* New York: Teachers College Press.

McIntosh, M. E., & Johnson, D. L. (1994). An instrument to facilitate communication between prospective team teachers. *Clearing House, 67*(3), 152-154.

Nicodemus, R. (1992). *Course teams.* East Lansing, MI: National Center for Research on Teacher Learning. (ERIC Document Reproduction Service No. ED346798)

Schoem, D. (Ed.). (1993). *Multicultural teaching in the university.* Westport, CT: Praeger.

Schwehn, M. N. (1993). *Exiles from Eden.* New York: Oxford University Press.

Weimer, M. (1993). *Improving your classroom teaching.* Thousand Oaks, CA: Sage.

Williams, J. A. (1994). *Classroom in conflict: Teaching controversial subjects in a diverse society.* Albany: State University of New York Press.

Chapter 10

Adams, D. M. (1990). *Cooperative learning and educational media: Collaborating with technology and each other.* Englewood Cliffs, NJ: Educational Technology Publications.

Beggs, D. W., III. (1964). Fundamental considerations for team teaching. In D. W. Beggs, III (Ed.), *Team teaching: Bold new venture* (pp. 29-50). Bloomington: Indiana University Press.

Bess, J. S. (Ed.). (1997). *Teaching well and liking it: Motivating faculty to teach effectively.* Baltimore: Johns Hopkins University Press.

Chamberlin, L. J. (1969). *Team teaching: Organization and administration.* Columbus, OH: Merrill.

Garmston, R. (1987). How administrators support peer coaching. *Educational Leadership, 44*(5), 18-26.

Garmston, R., Lindner, C., & Whitaker, J. (1993). Reflections on cognitive coaching. *Educational Leadership, 51*(2), 57-61.

George, P. G. (1995). *College teaching abroad.* Needham Heights, MA: Allyn & Bacon.

Katz, J. (1993). *Turning professors into teachers: A new approach to faculty development and student learning.* Phoenix, AZ: Oryx.

Kent, K. M. (1985). A successful program of teachers assisting teachers. *Educational Leadership, 43*(3), 30-33.

LaFauci, H. M., & Richter, P. E. (1970). *Team teaching at the college level.* New York: Pergamon.

Leggett, D., & Hoyle, S. (1987). Preparing teachers for collaboration. *Educational Leadership, 44,* 358-363.

Maeroff, G. I. (1993). *Team building for school change.* New York: Teachers College Press.

McIntosh, M. E., & Johnson, D. L. (1994). An instrument to facilitate communication between prospective team teachers. *Clearing House, 67*(3), 152-154.

Neubert, G. A., & Bratton, E. C. (1987). Team coaching: Staff development side by side. *Educational Leadership, 44*(5), 29-33.

Raywid, M. A. (1993). Finding time for collaboration. *Educational Leadership, 51*(1), 30-35.

Saxe, S. (1986). *The effect of peer interaction and incentive on adult learner achievement.* San Francisco: University of San Francisco, School of Education.

Showers, B. (1980). Improving inservice training: The messages of research. *Educational Leadership, 37*(5), 379-385.

Showers, B. (1982). *Transfer of training: The contribution of coaching.* Eugene, OR: Center for Educational Policy and Management.

Showers, B. (1984). *Peer coaching: A strategy for facilitating transfer of training.* Eugene, OR: Center for Educational Policy and Management.

Showers, B. (1995). *Student achievement through staff development: Fundamentals of school renewal.* White Plains, NY: Longman.

Showers, B., & Joyce, B. (1996). The evolution of peer coaching. *Educational Leadership, 53*(6), 12-17.

Chapter 11

Barnard, C. I. (1938). *The functions of the executive.* Cambridge, MA: Harvard University Press.

Boyer, E. L., Altbach, P. G., & Whitelaw, M. J. (1994). *Academic profession: An international perspective.* Princeton, NJ: Carnegie Foundation for the Advancement of Teaching.

Bruffee, K. A. (1993). *Collaborative learning: Higher education, interdependence, and the authority of knowledge.* Baltimore: Johns Hopkins University Press.

Cardozier, V. R. (1993). *Important lessons from innovative colleges and universities.* San Francisco: Jossey-Bass.

Centra, J. A. (1993). *Reflective faculty evaluations: Enhancing teaching and determining faculty effectiveness.* San Francisco: Jossey-Bass.

Chamberlin, L. J. (1969). *Team teaching: Organization and administration.* Columbus, OH: Merrill.

Dallman-Jones, A. S., & the Black River Group. (1994). *Handbook of effective teaching and assessment strategies.* Rockport, MA: Twin Lights.

Drake, S. M. (1993). *Planning integrated curriculum: The call to adventure.* Alexandria, VA: Association for Supervision and Curriculum Development.

Hallinger, P., Leithwood, K., & Murphy, J. (Eds.). (1993). *Cognitive perspectives on educational leadership.* New York: Teachers College Press.

Joyce, B. R. (1996). *Models of teaching.* Boston: Allyn & Bacon.

Joyce, B. R., Brown, C. C., Peck, L., & Butler, L. (Eds.). (1981). *Flexibility in teaching: An excursion into the nature of teaching and training.* New York: Longman.

Kent, K. M. (1985). A successful program of teachers assisting teachers. *Educational Leadership, 43*(3), 30-33.

Lopossa, B. D. (1971). *A comparative study of team and individual decision making.* Palo Alto, CA: Stanford Center for Research and Development in Teaching.

Maeroff, G. I. (1993). *Team building for school change.* New York: Teachers College Press.

Molnar, S. R. F. (1971). *Teachers in teams: Interaction, influence, and autonomy.* Palo Alto, CA: Stanford Center for Research and Development in Teaching.

Molnar, S. R. F. (1972). *The analysis of teachers' task contributions to decision-making interaction: Differences in three content areas and two types of teaching teams.* Palo Alto, CA: Stanford Center for Research and Development in Teaching.

Neubert, G. A., & Bratton, E. C. (1987). Team coaching: Staff development side by side. *Educational Leadership, 44*(5), 29-33.

Trousdale, A. M., & Henkin, R. (1991). Reflection on negotiating curriculum: Praxis in the language arts curriculum. *Teaching Education, 4*(1), 175-180.

Chapter 12

Angelo, T. A., & Cross, K. P. (1993). *Classroom assessment techniques: A handbook for college teachers.* San Francisco: Jossey-Bass.

Bair, M., & Woodward, R. G. (1964). *Team teaching in action.* Boston: Houghton-Mifflin.

Bess, J. S. (Ed.). (1997). *Teaching well and liking it: Motivating faculty to teach effectively.* Baltimore: Johns Hopkins University Press.

Bloom, B. S. (Ed.). (1955). *Taxonomy of educational objectives: The classification of educational goals: Handbook I. Cognitive domain.* New York: Longmans, Green.

Bowen, H. R., Clecak, P., Doud, J. P., & Douglass, G. K. (1977). *Investment in learning: The individual and social value of American higher education.* San Francisco: Jossey-Bass.

Braskamp, L. A., Brandenburg, D. C., & Ory, J. C. (1984). *Evaluating teaching effectiveness: A handbook.* Beverly Hills, CA: Sage.

Brown, S., & Race, P. (1995). *Assess your own teaching quality.* London: Kogan Page.

Chamberlin, L. J. (1969). *Team teaching: Organization and administration.* Columbus, OH: Merrill.

Counelis, J. S. (1978). *Technological culture and the human prospect.* San Francisco: University of San Francisco.

Crossman, D. M., & Behrens, S. G. (1992). *Affective strategies for effective learning.* East Lansing, MI: National Center for Research on Teacher Learning. (ERIC Document Reproduction Service No. ED344573)

Davis, H. S. (1966). *How to organize an effective team teaching program.* Englewood Cliffs, NJ: Prentice Hall.

Everhart, R. B. (1977). Role development and organizational change. *Journal of Research and Development in Education, 10*(2), 77-86.

Hammons-Bryner, S., & Robinson, B. (1994). Excitement in core curriculum courses. *College Teaching, 42*(3), 97-100.

Hanslovsky, G., Moyer, S., & Wagner, H. (1969). *Why team teaching?* Columbus, OH: Charles E. Merrill.

Harrow, A. J. (1977). *A taxonomy of the psychomotor domain: A guide for developing behavioral objectives.* New York: David McKay.

Hyman, R. T. (1970). *Ways of teaching.* Philadelphia: J. B. Lippincott.

Katz, J. (1993). *Turning professors into teachers: A new approach to faculty development and student learning.* Phoenix, AZ: Oryx.

Kilinski, K. K. (1973). *Organization and leadership in the local church.* Grand Rapids, MI: Zondervan.

Kratwohl, D. R., Bloom, B. S., & Masia, B. B. (1964). *Taxonomy of educational objectives: The classification of educational goals: Handbook II. Affective domain.* New York: David McKay.

Lyman, L. (1987). *Clinical instruction and supervision for accountability.* Dubuque, IA: Kendall/Hunt.

Mager, R. F. (1984). *Goal analysis.* Belmont, CA: Lake.

Mager, R. F. (1984). *Preparing instructional objectives.* Belmont, CA: Lake.

Mansell, J. (1974). Team-teaching in further education. *Educational Research, 17*(1), 19-26.

McIntosh, M. E., & Johnson, D. L. (1994). An instrument to facilitate communication between prospective team teachers. *Clearing House, 67*(3), 152-154.

Meredith, G. M. (1977). Toward a brief scale to measure the impact of team-teaching at the collegiate level. *Perceptual and Motion Skills, 44*(1), 242.

Nead, M. J. (1995). A team-taught business course: A case study of its effectiveness at a comprehensive community college. *Business Education Forum, 49*(3), 33-35.

Olivero, J. L. (1964). Evaluation considerations for team teaching. In D. W. Beggs, III (Ed.), *Team teaching: Bold new venture* (pp. 104-117). Bloomington: Indiana University Press.

Page, B. (1992, Spring). Evaluating, improving, and rewarding teaching: A case for collaboration. *ADE Bulletin,* No. 101, pp. 15-18.

Showers, B. (1980). Improving inservice training: The messages of research. *Educational Leadership, 37,* 379-385.

Showers, B. (1982). *Transfer of training: The contribution of coaching.* Eugene, OR: Center for Educational Policy and Management.

Showers, B. (1984). *Peer coaching: A strategy for facilitating transfer of training.* Eugene, OR: Center for Educational Policy and Management.

Showers, B. (1995). *Student achievement through staff development: Fundamentals of school renewal.* White Plains, NY: Longman.

Showers, B., & Joyce, B. (1996). The evolution of peer coaching. *Educational Leadership, 53*(6), 12-17.

Snow, C. P. (1961). *The two cultures and the scientific revolution.* New York: Cambridge University Press.

Weigand, J. (1971). *Developing teacher competencies.* Englewood Cliffs, NJ: Prentice Hall.

Weimer, M. (1993). *Improving your classroom teaching.* Thousand Oaks, CA: Sage.

Chapter 13

Amidon, E., & Hunter, E. (1966). *Improving teaching: The analysis of classroom verbal interaction.* New York: Holt, Rinehart, & Winston.

Anderson, M. (1992). *Imposters in the temple.* New York: Simon & Schuster.

Angelo, T. A., & Cross, K. P. (1993). *Classroom assessment techniques: A handbook for college teachers.* San Francisco: Jossey-Bass.

Braskamp, L. A., Brandenburg, D. C., & Ory, J. C. (1984). *Evaluating teaching effectiveness: A handbook.* Beverly Hills, CA: Sage.

Chamberlin, L. J. (1969). *Team teaching: Organization and administration.* Columbus, OH: Merrill.

Cunningham, R. T. (1971). Developing question-asking skills. In J. Weigand (Ed.), *Developing teacher competencies* (pp. 81-130). Englewood Cliffs, NJ: Prentice Hall.

Davis, B. G. (1993). *Tools for teaching.* San Francisco: Jossey-Bass.

Dunn, D. S. (1993). *What a psychologist learned by teaching writing: Improving technique and assessment.* East Lansing, MI: National Center for Research on Teacher Learning. (ERIC Document Reproduction Service No. ED365403)

Eble, K. E. (1988). *The craft of teaching: A guide to mastering the professor's art.* San Francisco: Jossey-Bass.

Elbow, P. (1986). *Embracing contraries: Explorations in learning and teaching.* New York: Oxford University Press.

Hyman, R. T. (1970). *Ways of teaching.* Philadelphia: J. B. Lippincott.

Johnson, D. W., Johnson, R. T., & Smith, K. A. (1991). *Cooperative learning: Increasing college faculty instructional productivity.* Washington, DC: George Washington University, School of Education and Human Development.

Johnson, R. H., Jr., & Hunt, J. J. (1968). *Rx for team teaching.* Minneapolis, MN: Burgess.

Katz, J. (1993). *Turning professors into teachers: A new approach to faculty development and student learning.* Phoenix, AZ: Oryx.

Lowman, J. (1984). *Mastering the techniques of teaching.* San Francisco: Jossey-Bass.

McIntosh, M. E., & Johnson, D. L. (1994). An instrument to facilitate communication between prospective team teachers. *Clearing House, 67*(3), 152-154.

Mothner, H. (1990). Students perform while teachers perfect their skills. *Education, 110,* 379-380.

Rosenholtz, S., & Kyle, S. (1984). Teacher isolation: Barrier to professionalism. *American Educator, 7,* 10-15.

Saxe, S. (1986). *The effect of peer interaction and incentive on adult learner achievement.* San Francisco: University of San Francisco, School of Education.

Showers, B., & Joyce, B. (1996). The evolution of peer coaching. *Educational Leadership, 53*(6), 12-17.

Weimer, M. (1993). *Improving your classroom teaching.* Thousand Oaks, CA: Sage.

Chapter 14

Adams, D. M. (1990). *Cooperative learning and educational media: Collaborating with technology and each other.* Englewood Cliffs, NJ: Educational Technology Publications.

Anderson, M. (1992). *Imposters in the temple.* New York: Simon & Schuster.

Bair, M., & Woodward, R. G. (1964). *Team teaching in action.* Boston: Houghton-Mifflin.

Beggs, D. W., III. (1964). *Team teaching: Bold new venture.* Bloomington: Indiana University Press.

Chamberlin, L. J. (1969). *Team teaching: Organization and administration.* Columbus, OH: Merrill.

Davis, B. G. (1993). *Tools for teaching.* San Francisco: Jossey-Bass.

Davis, H. S. (1966). *How to organize an effective team teaching program.* Englewood Cliffs, NJ: Prentice Hall.

Gage, N. L., & Travers, R. M. W. (1972). *Teacher effectiveness and teacher education: The search for a scientific basis.* Palo Alto, CA: Pacific Books.

Gage, N. L., & Travers, R. M. W. (Eds.). (1973). *Second handbook of research on teaching.* Chicago: Rand-McNally.

Garmston, R. (1987). How administrators support peer coaching. *Educational Leadership, 44*(5), 18-26.

Hanslovsky, G., Moyer, S., & Wagner, H. (1969). *Why team teaching?* Columbus, OH: Charles E. Merrill.

Johnson, R. H., Jr., & Hunt, J. J. (1968). *Rx for team teaching.* Minneapolis, MN: Burgess.

Kruger, L. J., Struzziero, J., Watts, R., & Vacca, D. (1995). The relationship between organizational support and satisfaction with teacher assistance teams. *Remedial and Special Education, 16,* 203-211.

LaFauci, H. M., & Richter, P. E. (1970). *Team teaching at the college level.* New York: Pergamon.

McIntosh, M. E., & Johnson, D. L. (1994). An instrument to facilitate communication between prospective team teachers. *Clearing House, 67*(3), 152-154.

Means, B. (1994). *Technology and education reform: The reality behind the promise.* San Francisco: Jossey-Bass.

Weimer, M. (1993). *Improving your classroom teaching.* Thousand Oaks, CA: Sage.

Chapter 15

Bair, M., & Woodward, R. G. (1964). *Team teaching in action.* Boston: Houghton-Mifflin.

Beggs, D. W., III. (Eds.). (1964). *Team teaching: Bold new venture.* Bloomington: Indiana University Press.

Chamberlin, L. J. (1969). *Team teaching: Organization and administration.* Columbus, OH: Merrill.

Gmelch, W. H. (1993). *Coping with faculty stress.* Thousand Oaks, CA: Sage.

Johnson, R. H., Jr., & Hunt, J. J. (1968). *Rx for team teaching.* Minneapolis, MN: Burgess.

Johnson, R. L. (1976). For the teacher's sake. *Colorado Journal of Educational Research, 16,* 60-62.

LaFauci, H. M., & Richter, P. E. (1970). *Team teaching at the college level.* New York: Pergamon.

Ornstein, A. C. (1982). Change and innovation in curriculum. *Journal of Research and Development in Education, 15*(2), 27-33.

Parker, G. M. (1990). *Team players and teamwork.* San Francisco: Jossey-Bass.

Reithlingshoefer, S. J. (1992). *The future of nontraditional/interdisciplinary programs: Margin or mainstream?* East Lansing, MI: National Center for Research on Teacher Learning. (ERIC Document Reproduction Service No. ED346789)

Weimer, M. (1993). *Improving your classroom teaching.* Thousand Oaks, CA: Sage.

Index

Accountability, 35-36
Action plan, 22
Administration, 15, 23, 34, 68, 82, 91
Advantages, 3-4, 11-15, 37, 80, 98-99
Aides, 5, 15, 37, 41-42, 92, 94
American Association of University
    Professors, 8
Analysis, 13, 29
Assessment. *See* Evaluation
Audiovisuals, 8, 15, 27, 67, 95. *See also*
    Technology

Bair, M., 5, 82, 93, 94
Boredom, 3, 8, 11, 13, 32, 80
Budget. *See* Financing

Capstone course, 48
CD-ROMs. *See* Technology, CD-ROMs
Change, 13, 15, 20, 68
Classroom:
    learning outside of, 30-31
    self-contained, 10
Class size, 10, 27, 34, 39, 94
Collaboration, 5, 6, 19, 38
Collaborative Leader, The (Sofield), 54
Communication, 5, 23, 29, 35, 54-55
Community-building, 66, 80
Compatibility, 37
Computers. *See* Technology, computers

Conflict:
    and interdisciplinary teams, 48
    and values, 60-61
    avoiding, 36-37
    benefits of, 59
    resolution, 48, 59-62
    results of, 59-61
    sources of, 35, 59-60
Content, 3, 4, 14, 29, 65
Coordinated teams. *See* Types of teams,
    coordinated
Corel 97, 88
Covey, Steven, 53-54
Creativity, 12, 42, 69
Critical thinking, 13, 29
Criticism, 38
Culture, 14, 19-20, 25-26, 35
Curriculum, 10, 20, 46, 47, 48

Decision making, 35, 38, 69-72
    and feedback, 72
    and objectivity, 70-71
    and subjectivity, 71
    styles of, 69
    systems approach to, 70-71
    See also Program design, and decision
    making
Definition, 3-5, 45
Democratic teams. *See* Types of teams,
    self-directed
Design. *See* Program design
Disadvantages, 13-15, 54, 99-100

123

About the Author

Francis J. Buckley, S.J., is Professor of Systematic and Pastoral Theology at the University of San Francisco. He received a doctorate in theology from the Gregorian University in Rome and did postdoctoral research in educational psychology at the University of Michigan. He has served as President of the College Theology Society in the United States and Canada and has taught in various countries at the elementary, secondary, undergraduate, and graduate levels, often offering team-taught courses that integrate theology and anthropology, communication arts, education, management, psychology, and sociology.